Employing that wickedly
exotic which distinguishe
History, Peter Bushell now
bizarre technicolour world

There are highly amusi
(who believed all babies are born with tails); of Jonas Hanway (who was convinced that tea drinking was a social evil leading to adultery, divorce and suicide); of Gladstone traipsing the streets of London in an endeavour to redeem fallen women; and of Squire Osbaldstone – that archetypal British eccentric – who defeated the French tennis champion using only his hand as a racquet; and saved an important cricket match by bowling in a drunken stupor whilst suffering from a broken shoulder.

In a world of increasing conformity, in which our individuality is being eroded almost daily, the proper study of mankind continues to be man. He is nowhere better displayed than here – in his crotchets.

Great ECCENTRICS

PETER BUSHELL

London
UNWIN PAPERBACKS
Boston Sydney

First published in Great Britain by George Allen & Unwin 1984
First published by Unwin Paperbacks 1985
Reprinted 1985

UNWIN ® PAPERBACKS
40 Museum Street, London WC1A 1LU, UK

Unwin Paperbacks
Park Lane, Hemel Hempstead, Herts HP2 4TE, UK

Allen & Unwin Inc.,
Fifty Cross Street, Winchester, Mass 01890, USA

George Allen & Unwin Australia Pty Ltd
8 Napier Street, North Sydney, NSW 2060, Australia

Unwin Paperbacks with the
Port Nicholson Press
PO Box 11–838 Wellington, New Zealand

0 04 827147 0

Set in 11 on 12½ point Garamond by Computape (Pickering) Ltd
and printed in Great Britain by Hazell Watson and Viney Ltd,
Member of the BPCC, Aylesbury, Bucks

This book is dedicated
to Anne, to Hilditch, to Lucy, and to Brave Little Teddy Lockett.
May none of them ever grow up

Author's Note

In a world of increasing conformity, in which our individuality is being eroded almost daily, the proper study of mankind continues to be man. He is nowhere more perfectly displayed than in his crotchets.

Eccentricity is not a modern phenomenon. Lincoln and Dogberry, Beethoven and Buddha were all touched by it; and Diogenes not only demonstrated his contempt for comfort but actually achieved some celebrity by living in a tub. Marching to the beat of a different drum, each in his way struck a deeply atavistic chord; revealing by his actions that which the rest of us so strenuously seek to disguise from ourselves: that every life is in some way a joke, and rather a good one.

The modern equivalent of the court jester, the eccentric teaches us the essential art of self-deflation. It is no easy matter and requires a certain amount of courage. As David Cort has remarked: 'Even the little child . . . who said that the Emperor had no clothes on must have had a nasty moment or two before everybody began laughing at himself.'

Within the modern meaning of the word, what follows cannot properly be termed history because history has rather lost its way. It has become pompous, profound and deeply self-absorbed. In consequence, the bulk of what we teach in our classrooms is hopelessly dull. It can never hope to touch the hearts or stir the minds of a generation devoted to the Big-Mac and the computerised game.

Contrary to popular belief, the past is not populated by statesmen, treaties and dates exclusively. It is also populated by exotic characters, strange and stirring events, long-forgotten jests and amusing gossip.

Great Eccentrics is an attempt to revive that aspect of our past. As with *London's Secret History*, I have endeavoured to tell my tale in an anecdotal way because, like Lord Orrery, I believe that anecdotes are like debts due to the public which every man, when he has that kind of cash about him, ought to pay.

Peter Bushell
London, January 1984

Acknowledgement

I would like to thank Hutchinsons for permission to publish the poem by J. B. S. Haldane entitled 'Cancer's A Funny Thing'.

Contents

Chapter 1

Actors Real and Imagined

Eccentricity is by nature democratic. It recognises no boundary and respects neither class nor creed. Because there are simply no firm criteria by which to measure it, this makes any study of it rather akin to beating quicksand with a stick. Like the demonic sprites of old, it adopts an endless series of disguises, investing everybody whom it touches with its own brand of sublime madness.

One of the most chameleon-like eccentrics was George Villiers, second Duke of Buckingham, who in a long life adopted many disguises. Born in 1627 – the year in which his father was assassinated at Portsmouth – he was brought up at Court with the children of Charles I. At the outbreak of the Civil War he rallied to the Royalist flag, supporting the cause with fierce loyalty. After the King's forces were defeated at the battle of Worcester he was obliged to go into hiding. He chose to do so not in some obscure part of the country but in London, walking about quite freely under the noses of his enemies. Having purchased a grotesque disguise and a mask, he adopted the name 'Jack Pudding', representing himself as a mummer and a singer of ballads. He also doubled as a quack doctor, peddling patent remedies.

He became an overnight sensation. People flocked to see him from every quarter of the capital. By electing to perform his tricks before Wallingford House, his own front door, he had chosen to live very dangerously. Yet his primary purpose was not to make his enemies look foolish but to establish contact with his sister, the beautiful Duchess of Richmond, then languishing under house arrest in the nearby Palace of Whitehall.

One day, the Duchess of Richmond obtained permission to pay a visit to her husband at Windsor. As her heavily guarded coach turned into Whitehall it was spotted by 'Jack Pudding', who jumped down from his perch and commanded it to stop. Anticipating some fun, the soldiers riding escort exchanged good-humoured grins and reined in their horses.

'Jack' walked up to the carriage and sang a satirical song about its occupant. He then sang another about her brother. At its conclusion, he raised his mask, and mockingly presented the lady with some broadsheets. Everyone assumed these to be copies of the songs. The Duchess retained her composure, hid her surprise and ordered the carriage to drive on. As it rattled away she was seen to throw the sheaf of papers at the head of her lady-in-waiting. She later found it contained a plan of escape.

'Jack Pudding's graceful figure and droll manner at last attracted the notice of Bridget Ireton, Oliver Cromwell's frosty daughter. Respectable, newly married and outwardly very staid, Bridget asked for a private interview. When Buckingham granted this she attempted to seduce him. He rejected her advances, claiming to be a devout Jew, forbidden to have congress with Christian women by Talmudic law. Bridget arranged a second interview, producing a Talmudic lawyer to dispute the point with him. Buckingham asked for time to consider. He sensibly avoided a third encounter – but once the need for maintaining the fiction had passed he was at pains to let the lady know the true identity of her reluctant suitor.

When his estates were assigned by parliament to Lord Fairfax, Buckingham retreated to France. In 1656 he secretly returned to

England and with characteristic impudence married Lord Fairfax's daughter, who as an only child was her father's heir. Four years later, Charles II was restored to the throne and Buckingham to his lands. He remained a leading figure of the Restoration court for a quarter of a century. In peace time his audacious gallantry and high bravado found an outlet in political intrigue and clandestine love affairs. In 1667 he was instrumental in bringing about the downfall of lord chancellor Clarendon; and the following year he killed in a duel the Earl of Shrewsbury. The Earl's wife – Buckingham's mistress – insisted on witnessing the encounter by disguising herself as a page-boy, standing impassively at the head of her lover's horse while her husband bled to death at her feet. The author, or part author, of several good plays, notably *The Rehearsal*, Buckingham eventually intrigued himself into disgrace, dying at the age of sixty, destitute and alone in what has been called 'the worst inn's worst room'.

Another turbulent aristocrat blessed with dramatic talent was the seventh Earl of Barrymore. He longed for fame as an actor and was not in truth a bad one, but his spirit was too restless to be fixed for long in any one course. He was either off riding to hounds, or fighting bare-knuckle, or chasing some rare piece of bloodstock, so that a review of his life is a catalogue of intense but short-lived passions akin to the preposterous enslavements of the Intelligent Mr Toad. He was very fond of picnics for a time, but even these had to incorporate an element of challenge. The servants were sent ahead to bury the food and the guests then amused themselves by hunting for it. Those who refused to play – or were simply no good – went hungry.

Barrymore's rakish ways earned him the nickname 'Hellgate'. His two brothers were respectively dubbed 'Newgate' – from being once detained in that prison – and 'Cripplegate' – on account of a physical deformity. All three were addicted to practical jokes, the most notorious of which involved placing flush to some rich man's door a coffin, balanced on end, containing a servant made up to look like a corpse. On one occasion this all but cost the servant his life. The housemaid who answered the door was so overcome by the gruesome sight confronting her that she fainted. Her master, who happened by chance to be following in her wake, discharged a pistol at the 'corpse', the bullet missing its mark by a hair's breadth.

In a sinister way, the incident prefigured the Earl's end, which occurred at the early age of twenty-three. Whilst on military service, he was detailed to escort a group of French prisoners to Dover. In the hope of a little duck hunting, he had a gun placed in his gig. The roads were bad and the jolting of the carriage caused the gun to slip. The trigger caught on a projection and the Earl received a mortal wound in the left eye, dying in half an hour.

Barrymore was often abominably rude to strangers, a characteristic which he shared with Jonathan Swift. One day, 'resting his bones in a coffee-house', Swift was accosted by Dr Arbuthnot who, having no idea who he was but being greatly amused by his singular manner and peculiar wardrobe, resolved to have some fun with him. He had been writing a letter, which he now held up still wet and asked: 'Pray, sir, have you any sand about you?' Swift looked at him for a moment and replied: 'No, sir, but I have the gravel* and if you will give me your letter I will piss upon it'. Despite this inauspicious beginning, the two men afterwards became good friends.

The son of a Dublin attorney, Jonathan Swift was born on 30th November 1667, two months after the death of his father. His constitution was never good and as a young man he thought to strengthen it by running half a mile up and down a hill every two hours. At the age of fourteen he was entered as a student at Trinity College, Dublin. He was neither dilligent nor happy in his studies and only obtained 'his degree by *special favour*, a term used in that university to denote want of merit'.

In the last year of the seventeenth century, Swift entered the church. He was appointed rector of Laracor, an Irish parish so deficient in Christian feeling that one service was attended only by himself and his clerk, Roger. Swift began his sermon: 'Dearly beloved Roger, the scriptures moveth you and me in sundry places'.

On the accession of Queen Anne, he repaired to London in hope of preferment. His curious appearance and whimsical manner earned him the title 'the mad parson'. Kicking his heels in search of a patron, he spent much of his time at Buttons coffee-house where 'it was his custom to lay his hat down on a table and walk to and fro at a good pace for half an hour or an hour, without speaking to any mortal, or seeming to attend in the least to any thing that was going forward'. At

* A disease which causes gravelly matter to accumulate in the bladder.

the end of this period he would settle his account and leave, having uttered not one word.

When he did choose to open his mouth the results were equally spectacular. One evening he approached a total stranger at Buttons and began, very abruptly: 'Pray, sir, do you remember any good weather in the world?' The stranger was rather taken aback, but after a moment replied: 'Yes, sir, I thank God, I remember a great deal of good weather in my time'. Swift said: 'That is more than I can say. I never remember any weather that was not too cold or too hot, too wet or too dry; but however God Almighty contrives it, at the end of the year 'tis all very well'. According to H. Wilson: 'On saying this, he took up his hat, and without uttering another word, or taking the least notice of anyone, walked out of the coffee-house, leaving all the spectators of this odd scene staring after him and still more confirmed in the opinion of his insanity'.

Amongst his other oddities, Swift counted a manic attachment to reckoning. He once remarked that he could cover the two miles from his rooms in Chelsea to the centre of London 'in just five thousand and seven hundred and forty-eight steps'.

This game has always been popular among the imaginative and superstitious and is especially favoured by the young. A mystical formula designed to placate the gods, it is sometimes called: 'If-I-can-hold-my-breath-until-I-reach-the-fourth-lamppost-it-will-be-chips-for-tea'. One man who played it in a literally roundabout way was Charles Parnell, the Irish politician. Walking home one day with Frank Harris, he reached the door of his house only to walk away again. A second approach was made and again he walked away. He explained to Harris that he always kept a mental count of the number of paces required to walk between any two points and could never bring himself to conclude a journey if the total contained either the number four or the number eight, both of which he considered held a sinister significance for him. Seven he thought a good number, while: 'Nine is a real symbol of good luck and I can go in rejoicing'.

In 1713 Swift was presented with the deanery of St Patrick's Cathedral and returned to Dublin. As soon as it could be decently arranged he came back to London, but on the death of Queen Anne again crossed the Irish Sea to commence what he always thought of as 'my life of exile'. He had a desperate love of a shilling and in consequence lived very frugally. Nonetheless, his fame was growing and his writings and public character soon caused him to become 'the idol of the populace'. Their blind faith in him was quite astounding. One day, when it was rumoured that there was to be an eclipse of the sun, a great number of people gathered in front of the Deanery to witness it. Their murmurings proving a distraction, Swift sent out the beadle who rang his bell and announced: 'Oyez! Oyez! It is the Dean of St Patrick's will and pleasure that the eclipse be put off until this hour tomorrow'. The crowd dispersed in high dudgeon, muttering that it should not return as a man who could once postpone an eclipse might easily do so again.

In political matters the Dean was a fearless champion of the poor. In 1724 a man named Wood contrived with the assistance of Ireland's rulers to put two hundred thousand pounds worth of small coin into circulation. Because of its minute copper content, this would in real terms have been practically worthless. Hearing of the plan, Swift stumped off to Dublin castle where, at the height of a levee, he publicly denounced the newly appointed lord lieutenant by saying: 'You have given a noble specimen of what this devoted country is to hope for from your government. I suppose you expect a statue of copper will be erected to you for this service done to Wood'.

Three years after this confrontation, Swift published *Gulliver's Travels*, which was received with 'such avidity that the price of the first addition was raised before the second could be prepared'. The book was mostly written at Quilca, where Swift for a time put up with his lifelong friend, Doctor Sheridan. During his sojourn, he made the acquaintance of a farmer named Reilly and one Sunday, after church, invited himself to dinner. Reilly's wife, a rather vain woman, became so excited at the prospect of having such an eminent fellow beneath her roof that she tricked herself out in her finest apparel.

On arriving at the house the good Dean '. . . saluted her with the same respect as if she had been a duchess, making several conges down to the ground, and then handed her with great formality to her seat'. After a period of polite but general chatter, Swift said: 'I suppose, Mr Reilly, you have a considerable estate here. Let us go and look over your demesne'. At this Reilly's mouth dropped open. 'Estate?' said he. 'Why, devil a foot of land belongs to me or any of my generation. I have a pretty good lease here indeed from Lord Fingal, but he threatens that he will not renew it and I have but a few years of it to come'.

The conversation moved on to other topics. But after about half an hour, Swift turned to his host and said: 'And when am I to see Mrs Reilly?' Reilly replied: 'Why, don't you see her there before you?' Swift said: 'That? Mrs Reilly? Impossible! I have heard she is a prudent woman, and as such would never dress herself out in silks, and other ornaments, fit only for ladies of fashion. No, Mrs Reilly, the farmer's wife, would never wear any thing better than plain stuff'.

Mrs Reilly took the hint and soon afterwards disappeared. When she returned she was dressed more modestly. Swift took her hand and said: 'I am heartily glad to see you, Mrs Reilly. This husband of yours would fain have palmed a fine lady upon me, all dressed out in silks, and in the pink of the mode, for his wife, but I was not to be taken in so'.

He next turned to Reilly's son and, taking a penknife, cut away the lace trimming from his hat which he threw into the fire. When it had been partially consumed, he fished it out, wrapped it in paper and tucked it into his pocket. The Reillys were too much in awe of him to complain at this singular behaviour; but just as he was leaving he produced the paper from his pocket and said: 'I do not intend to rob you, Mrs Reilly. I shall take nothing belonging to you away with me. There's your son's hat lace. I have only changed the form of it to a much better one'. After he had departed, Mrs Reilly unwrapped the paper. In addition to the burned lace, it contained four guineas. On his return to Dublin, Swift made a point of seeking out Lord Fingal and persuading him to renew Reilly's lease.

He demonstrated a similar consideration towards his own servants who were invariably selected by his housekeeper, Mrs Whiteway. Once they had been hired, Swift had them into his study and announced that he asked only two things of them: one was to shut the door after them when they came into a room; the other was to shut it again on leaving. One day a maidservant approached him and requested leave to attend the wedding of her sister. Swift readily concurred. Learning that the wedding was to take place that very day in a small village about ten miles from Dublin, he concluded that this was too great a distance for the girl to walk in the time and loaned her one of his horses. The maidservant was so overcome that on quitting his presence for the stables she inadvertantly left the door ajar. In about a quarter of an hour, Swift ordered a second horse to be saddled and sent a servant after her to bring her back. She entered the room quaking with fright and wondering what she could have done to offend him. Swift said: 'Child, you forgot to shut the door'. Having said which he allowed her to resume her journey.

This peculiar blend of kindness and irascibility led Swift into numerous scrapes; but it masked an extraordinarily sensitive disposition. During his residence in London, John Gay and Alexander Pope called on him one evening unexpectedly. Pope records that:

> On our coming in, 'Heyday, gentlemen', says the doctor, 'what's the meaning of this visit? How come you to leave all the great lords you are so fond of, to come hither to see a poor dean?' 'Because we would rather see you than any of them.' 'Ay, any one who does not know you as well as I do might believe you. But since you are come, I must get some supper for you, I suppose?' 'No, doctor, for we have supped already.' 'Supped already? That's impossible! Why, 'tis not eight o'clock yet.' 'Indeed we have.' 'That's very strange; but if you had not supped, I must have got something for you. Let me see, what should I have had? A couple of lobsters? Ay, that would have done very well – two shillings: tarts – a shilling. But you will drink a glass of wine with me, though you supped so much before your usual time, only to spare my pocket?' 'No; we would rather talk with you than drink with you.' 'But if you had supped with me – as in all reason you ought to have done – you must have drank with me. A bottle of wine – two shillings. Two and two is four and one is five. Just two and sixpence apiece. There, Pope, there's half a crown for you; and there's another for you, sir: for I won't save anything by you, I am determined'.

Pope concludes: 'This was all said and done with his usual seriousness . . . and in spite of every thing we could say to the contrary, he actually obliged us to take the money'.

Separated from Swift in time, if not in spirit, is another eccentric churchman, the Reverend Sydney Smith. Swift's oddness permeated every aspect of his being. Sydney was peculiar only in his conversation. Like Swift, he adored every aspect of London, but was forced by circumstances to live for long periods in the country, which he thought 'a kind of healthy grave'. He found its pursuits unfathomable and once said: 'When I take a gun in my hand I am sure the safest place for a pheasant is just opposite the muzzle'.

Unlike the witty eccentrics who came after him – Wilde and Harris and Tree – whose *bon mots* are still relished and repeated, the essence of Sydney's eccentricity has not endured, perhaps because his sallies were the momentary extension of the man. It was the *spirit* of his conversation – and the ludicrous gestures and extravagant drollness of expression which punctuated it – that made his company so irresistible. When Sydney was in full flow 'the servants fled from the room with tears running down their faces' and Thomas Smith almost choked to death on his mutton.

One of Sydney's regular guests was the great tragedienne, Sarah Siddons, whom he said 'never got out of tragedy even in private life. She used to *stab* her potatoes; and said, "Boy, give me a knife!" as she would have said on the stage, "Give me a dagger."'

When Mrs Siddons held 'at homes' she would sometimes condescend to amuse her guests by reading pasages from Shakespeare – although the account left us by Benjamin Robert Haydon, the historical painter, suggests that amusement hardly entered into it:

> while we were all eating toast and tingling cups and saucers she began again. Immediately, like the effect of a Mass bell at Madrid, all noise ceased and we slunk away to our seats like boys, two or three of the most distinguished men of the day with very great bits of toast sticking out their cheeks, afraid to bite. It was curious to see [Sir Thomas] Lawrence . . . his cheek swelled from his mouth being full . . . to hear him bite by degrees, and then stop for fear of making too much crackle, while his eyes full of water told the torture he was in; at the same moment you heard Mrs S. say: 'eye of newt, toe of frog', then Lawrence gave a sly bite and pretended to be awed and listening. It was too exquisite!

For comedy, Mrs Siddons had no aptitude. As Fanny Burney shrewdly noted: 'gaiety sits not naturally upon her – it seems more like disguised gravity'. Her presence was so imposing that Sheridan once said: 'Make love to Mrs Siddons? I would as soon have thought of making love to the Archbishop of Canterbury'. Yet Sydney Smith once reduced her to such a state of helpless mirth that she developed an acute attack of the hiccups and had to be helped from the house.

Characteristically, 'darling Sydney' reserved his best remarks for his death-bed. He had long been a martyr to the gout, the pain of which he likened to 'walking on my eyeballs'; and to Lady Carlisle he wrote: 'I look as if a curate has been taken out of me'. To another correspondent he confessed: 'I feel so weak both in body and mind that I verily believe, if the knife were put into my hand, I should not have strength or energy enough to slide it into a Dissenter'. When Lord Houghton visited him and asked what kind of a night he had passed, Sydney replied: 'Oh, horrid, horrid, my dear fellow. I dreamed I was chained to a rock and being talked to death by Harriett Martineau and Macaulay'. On 22nd February 1845, thinking he might have swallowed some ink in mistake for his medicine, he laughingly told a servant to 'bring me all the blotting paper there is in the house'. The girl took him at his word. Before she could return he was dead.

A third cleric who heartily detested the country and grasped every opportunity to escape from it was 'Jumbo' Davidson, the eccentric

Rector of Stiffkey. Good looking and dapper, but somewhat short and cursed with a high squeaky voice, 'Jumbo Davidson' was descended from a long line of protestant clergymen. After an early career as a comic, during which he gave recitals somewhat after the manner of the senior George Grossmith, he entered the church. Following a series of minor but nonetheless significant adventures he was appointed rector of the Norfolk village of Stiffkey (pronounced 'Stewkey'). He performed his duties adequately; but as one of the villagers recalled, half a century after his death, he never really took to the life: 'He loved London. He was too clever for a country lane'.

Davidson's downfall was caused by a fatal weakness for pretty girls. He accosted them wherever he went. In some cases he claimed to be rescuing them from a life of sin. Others were to be 'discovered' for the stage. With his Homburg planted squarely on his head, and puffing on a sixpenny cigar, he would slip away to London, approach the first pretty girl he encountered and ask: 'Are you not Miss ———, the famous actress?' The girl never was, but the ice had been broken and he was soon offering to use his theatrical connections to get her a job on the boards. He sometimes succeeded.

'Jumbo' Davidson was almost certainly driven by a sincere desire to be of help; but his superiors were the first to realise that this was not his primary motivation and they decided to unfrock him. The Rector struck back by composing an emotional and badly written plea for understanding which appeared on the front page of The *Empire News* under the banner headline: 'I Challenge My Traducers'.

The case was heard at Church House, Westminster, in 1932. Davidson argued that he was a kindly, erratic but well-meaning eccentric: his association with low women had been misrepresented and misunderstood. Had not Mr Gladstone often talked to prostitutes in the hope of leading them to salvation? The analogy was not acceptable and in the October Harold Davidson was ritually unfrocked in the cloisters of Norwich cathedral. He invested the proceedings with an element of farce by arriving an hour late and wilfully overturning the hallowed order of precedence by marching to the high altar in front of the bishop.

Davidson now set out to hit the headlines in earnest. He did so for several reasons, all of them financial. He had a wife and a sizeable family. His stipend of eight hundred a year had ceased with his unfrocking and the rectory was required by the new incumbent. He may also have been motivated by a strong sense of injustice. He firmly believed that the Consistory Court had brought him low because he had refused to conform to their standards of behaviour. But its members were not judges, the 'trial' had no real validity, and he had broken no law. He had nonetheless been deprived of his livelihood.

He calculated that the best way to be revenged was to cease to be eccentric and become utterly outrageous. To this end he preached from the mouth of a stuffed whale and sat in a side-show booth, the walls of which were papered with his press cuttings, importuning the paying public with a list of his grievances. He next announced his intention of fasting to death, naked, in a barrel. Suicide, or its attempt, was then still a criminal offence and he was arrested. The jury found him not guilty. The Rector sued the authorities for wrongful arrest and was awarded damages of three hundred and eighty-two pounds.

In the summer of 1937 he appeared at Skegness, fulminating against the elders of the church from the centre of a large cage which he shared with a fearsome looking lion. One day the lion turned and mauled him. 'Jumbo' was taken to hospital where on 30th July 1937 – the day another buffoon, King Farouk, was crowned in Egypt – he died.

The Times printed his obituary – although, as Malcolm Muggeridge has pointed out: 'he would scarcely have had an obituary at all if he had not been unfrocked, starved in a barrel and thrown to circus lions'. On the day of his funeral, people descended on Stiffkey from all parts of the country, many of them in charabancs. Squads of police had to be employed to hold them back. His widow caused a minor sensation by arriving for the ceremony dressed all in white – white shoes, white stockings, white hat, white dress. When someone asked her why she had eschewed the traditional colour of mourning, she smiled – and pointed to her black shoe laces.

One of the theatrical impresarios whom Davidson pestered in his efforts to get his girls on the stage was the actor-manager, Sir Herbert Beerbohm Tree. He came so regularly that Tree took to muttering: 'Oh, no, not you again', slamming the door in his face. He must have been a great trial because in the normal way Tree was the most approachable of men. The corridor outside his office was crowded night and day with out-of-work actors, hopeful playwrights and that mixed bag of spongers and seekers after patronage which surrounds every successful man. Sir Herbert saw them all – and very strange encounters some of them proved. One hopeful actress kept an appointment wearing a hat decorated by a stuffed bird. Sir Herbert stroked it. Being rather in awe of him, the young woman was too timid to risk raising her head and Sir Herbert continued to stroke the bird throughout the interview. The poor girl suffered agonies of cramp and came to a subsequent meeting bareheaded. 'Hello', said Tree. 'Where's the bird?'

At the turn of the century Tree built Her Majesty's Theatre in the Haymarket, installing himself in a suite of private apartments beneath the dome. Here he gave magnificent dinner parties which became known as 'Sir Herbert Tree's At Domes'. A frequent guest at these was his half-brother, the artist and writer, Max Beerbohm. The two men were markedly different in character and one night an observer said that they appeared to exist 'in an attitude of armed neutrality'. 'No,' said Max, 'terrified love.' In fact they understood one another perfectly. On another occasion, Max was asked why his brother had chosen to use the name Tree. Max explained that Beerbohm in German meant 'pear tree'. 'He also had the prescience to realise that "we want Tree" is a great deal less difficult for an audience than "we want Beerbohm".'

Under Tree's management, Her Majesty's was equipped with every possible convenience and gadget, including a lift which transported the great man from his quarters in the dome to the stage. One day, as he was descending to make his entrance, it stuck. Seeing the panic-stricken stage hands running about below, he called down: 'send on a procession'. It is probable that he was thinking of one of those 'mind's-eye processions of popes, jugglers and sinister servants holding peacocks in the leash' which were said by his daughter to have passed continuously through his head 'to the accompaniment of music, sad strange and grotesque'.

The last of the true amateurs, Tree was surpassed as a master of stagecraft only by Sir Henry Irving. But while Irving was playing it safe at the Lyceum, in copper-bottomed successes and supported by casts which he knew could never outshine him, Tree – who cared nothing for being upstaged – was producing all manner of perilous and innovative work at Her Majesty's.

Nonetheless, Irving always remained the more popular man, as Sir Herbert one day found to his cost. On a visit to Claude Lowther's family seat, Herstmonceux Castle, he was walking with his host in the grounds when a party of day-trippers asked if they might look over the gardens. Claude Lowther – known from his extravagant manner of dress as 'Loud Clother' – pointed to Tree and said: 'Well, you know, you must ask Mr Lowther'. Sir Herbert graciously granted permission – adding that they should help themselves to apples from the orchard. Not to be outdone, Lowther introduced himself as Sir Herbert Tree and offered them free seats at 'his' theatre. Their leader said: 'Very kind of you, guv'nor. But I don't suppose you could get us in to see 'enry Irving instead?'

For all this, Tree was unquestionably one of the finest actors of the nineteenth century. His portrayal of *Svengali*, which exactly suited his strong and imperious character, has been described by the *Encyclopaedia Britannica* as 'perhaps the best individual performance ever seen'. It also unwittingly popularised a new form of headgear: the trilby hat.

In certain roles, however, the great man was abysmal; and on one occasion, when a performance of *Hamlet* was brought to a standstill by a tempest of hissing and boos, he walked to the footlights and held up both hands for silence. He knew that it is hopeless to try to defend oneself on such occasions. Only *hubris* will suffice. Tree said: 'Thank you, ladies and gentlemen. I still have a few pearls to cast'.

Of other people's productions he was a harsh critic. Looking round backstage during a performance of *Hamlet*, in which his son was playing the title role, he noticed a brazier on the castle ramparts and snorted: 'I see the streets are up in Elsinore'. In 1916, when the musical extravaganza *Chu Chin Chow* came to Her Majesty's he dismissed it as 'scented hogwash', describing the scanty costumes as 'more navel than millinery'.

In twenty years under Sir Herbert Tree, Her Majesty's put on more than fifty plays. Thanks to the owner's magical influence and magnetic personality, most of them made money. It was an influence which pervaded every aspect of production. One day, during a rehearsal for *Macbeth*, the great man found himself interrupted in full flow by an uncued clap of thunder. Shading his eyes with his hands, he peered into the auditorium. In a frosty voice, he said: 'When I require the assistance of the sound-effects department, you may be sure that I shall ask for it'. After a moment's pause, a disembodied voice replied: 'I think you will find that was real thunder, Sir Herbert'. 'Ah' said Tree, pensively. 'I thought it wasn't as good as ours.'

Tree was fundamentally a Victorian and found certain aspects of Edwardian life very frightening. He had a morbid dread of motor cars and continued to use horse-drawn transport almost to the end of his days. When he did at last consent to ride in a car it proved a terrifying experience. He slid almost at once to the floor and remained there for the duration of the journey, viewing the passing scenery from between his fingers.

With this one exception, there was almost no situation over which he did not have instant and complete command. One day he encountered a man struggling down the Haymarket hugging an enormous long-case clock. He said: 'My dear man, why not carry a watch?'

If his wit betrayed him it was in a weakness for mock-Confucian epigrams, the worst of which would not have disgraced a match-box. 'Life and death hinge on the letter "m": without it we have creation; insert it and we have cremation.' 'Let sleeping dogs lie, but why let lying dogs sleep?' Perhaps the best was: 'If you drink too much wine you get drunk. If you drink too much water you get drowned'.

For Sir Herbert Beerbohm Tree, creation ended in cremation in 1917. His ashes were interred in Hampstead Cemetery. He left a moderate fortune of £44,000 and several illegitimate children. One of these was the film director, Sir Carol Reed. Another became the father of the screen actor, Oliver Reed. If we are to believe Ken Russell, Sir Herbert's grandson has not inherited his talent. 'Oliver' says Russell 'has three methods of acting: Moody One, Moody Two and Moody Three'.

An equally witty theatrical eccentric, but one who lacked Tree's command of money, was Richard Brinsley Sheridan, who in 1776 headed a triumvirate which acquired the patent of the Theatre Royal, Drury Lane, from David Garrick at a cost of £80,000. Three years later, Sheridan's last dramatic composition, *The Critic*, was produced here. Unfortunately, the author was already preoccupied with his political career and, as Michael Kelly recorded in his *Reminiscences*, the last scene had still not been written two days prior to the opening night. Sheridan's partners became extremely nervous and the actors were in a state of despair, 'especially King, who was not only stage-manager, but had to play Puff'.

King sought Sheridan out and demanded to know whether the piece would be finished in time. Sheridan said it would – and rushed off to the House of Commons. In a state of despair, King confided his anxieties to Mr Linley who, being Sheridan's father-in-law, and 'pretty well aware of his habits, hit upon a stratagem. A night rehearsal of *The Critic* was ordered and Sheridan, having dined with Linley, was prevailed upon to go. While they were on the stage, King whispered [to] Sheridan that he had something particular to communicate, and begged that he would step into the second green-room.'

Sheridan agreed and was pleasantly surprised to find that the fire had been made up; that a dish of anchovies and two bottles of claret had been placed on the table; that there was a good armchair; and a plentiful supply of pens, ink and paper. While Sheridan was surveying the scene, King quietly removed himself from the room and locked the door. Shortly afterwards, Sheridan's two partners came up and announced that until such time as he had completed the last act, the playwright must consider himself their prisoner.

According to Michael Kelly: 'Sheridan took this decided measure in good part; he ate the anchovies, finished the claret, wrote the scene and laughed heartily at the ingenuity of the contrivance'. It would have been a miracle had he left the claret. Like Richard Porson, he was a compulsive drinker who hardly cared what he consumed so long as it possessed a degree of alcohol. In 1795, when his doctor visited him at his house in Hertford Street, he warned him that 'the brandy Arquebusade* and eau-de-cologne he swallowed would burn off the coat of his stomach'. Sheridan replied: 'Then my stomach must digest in its waistcoat, for I cannot help it'.

Nor, it seems, could he help his perennial poverty. As a result of his reckless gambling he was always behind with his rent and one landlord was driven to limit his indebtedness by removing the roof. He was also permanently beholden to the moneylender, 'Jew' King, who profited so handsomely by the excesses of men such as Sheridan that he was able to keep a superb coach stationed before his house in Clarges Street 'attended by two spruce footmen in striking but not

* A prophylactic mixture used at that date for the treatment of bullet wounds.

gaudy livery, with long canes in their hands'. The coachman 'was apparelled in a coat of many capes, a powdered wig and gloves *à la Henri Quatre*'.

Small wonder that when the playwright was informed that the two 'lost' tribes of Israel had been found he retorted. 'I am very glad to hear it as I have very nearly exhausted the other ten'. When he remarked to his son, Tom, that the family name had formerly been O'Sheridan, but that the 'O' had afterwards been dropped, the lad said he could not think why: 'We owe everybody'.

A short time later, when Tom announced that he intended to follow his father into politics, Sheridan revenged himself for this slight. Being something of an idealist, the lad announced that, unlike his father, he would commit himself to no faction on a regular basis but vote on each issue according to his conscience. Tapping his forehead, he said: 'I shall hang here a sign saying This Space To Let'. Sheridan said: 'Then you had best add "with vacant possession"'.

In 1791 and with no source of revenue but his theatre, Sheridan commissioned Henry Holland to enlarge it. The work took three years and the end product was a model of elegance and modernity. The stage, the largest London had ever seen, was protected by a huge metal safety curtain. As a further precaution against fire, two capacious reservoirs were installed on the roof. In an age of ebullient invention, these were relatively conservative security devices. A rival theatre was equipped with a burglar alarm which emitted a dog-like bark on the opening of an exterior door and a fire engine which played 'Home Sweet Home' as it doused the roof above.

The renovations had plunged Sheridan even further into debt; and Gronow relates that one night the treasurer sought the playwright out in the wings:

> with a woefully long face, and told him that there was not enough money to pay even the subordinates on the following day; and that unless a certain sum could be found he was persuaded that the house could not open on the Monday. Sheridan suggested several plans for raising the wind, but all were declared by Mr Dunn to be useless. Sheridan gazed round at the thinly-peopled boxes, and at length called to one of the porters in waiting 'Do you see that stout, good-tempered looking man seated next a comely lady in the third

box from the stage, in a front row? Immediately the play is over, go to him; have a couple of wax candles carried by a boy who can make graceful bows; open the box door, and in a loud voice enough to be heard by every one say, "Sir, Mr Sheridan requests *the honour of a private interview* with you in his own room". Let every one on the way treat him with the greatest civility; and, Mr Dunn, will you have the kindness to see that a bottle of the best port and a couple of wine glasses are placed on the table in my study.'

The reason for this preference was simple. As the standing member for Stafford, Sheridan had recognised the man as one of his more prosperous constituents.

'The order was duly obeyed. The gentleman was ushered into the presence of Sheridan with honours almost approaching those shown to royalty, and was received by him with the most cordial marks of friendship and regard.'

The playwright poured his victim a glass of port. After a moment or two, he said: 'I am always happy to see any one from Stafford. I am glad that you called at my house for an order to this theatre, where I hope you will come when you please. You will find your name on the free list. I think I remember you told me you came twice a year to London'. The man confirmed that this was so: 'to receive my dividends'.

Gronow continues:

'Ah,' said the manager, 'you are in Consols, whilst I, alas, am Reduced and can get nothing till April, when, you know, the interest is paid; and till then I shall be in great distress.' 'Oh,' said his constituent, 'let not that make you uneasy; if you give me the power of attorney to receive the money for you when it is due, I can let you have three hundred pounds, which I shall not want till then.' 'Only a real friend' said Sheridan, shaking his dupe by the hand with warmth 'could have made such a proposition. I accept it thankfully.' And the three hundred pounds were immediately transferred from the pocket book of the unwary man of Stafford into that of the penniless manager of the theatre.

In April, when the power of attorney was presented to Sheridan for signature, he said: 'I never spoke of Consols *in* Reduced, I only spoke of my Consols *being* reduced; unhappy is the man who does not comprehend the weight of prepositions.'

Burning with righteous indignation:

> the man from Stafford rushed up to London and found his cajoler seated in his room at Drury Lane. Sheridan, apparently not at all disconcerted, with outstretched hand and benignant smile, welcomed his victim, whose rage was at first uncontrollable; but his attack was met by the manager with an acknowledgement that, in a moment of urgent necessity he had been compelled to throw himself on the generosity of a man who he had heard from every one was a model of worth and whose acquaintance would be acceptable in the highest quarters.

Pulling on his coat, he said:

> 'But excuse me, my dear sir, I am now commanded to go to the Prince of Wales, to whom I shall narrate your noble conduct. My carriage is waiting and I can take you to Carlton House.' The eye of the provincial sparkled with delight. Was it possible that he meant to take him to the Prince of Wales? It sounded something like it. He shook Sheridan by the hand, saying: 'I forgive you, my dear friend; never mention the debt again'. 'I will take care never to do so,' said the manager. The carriage came round to the door, the two friends entered it, and when they arrived at Carlton House, Sheridan got out, and closing the door, told the coachman to drive the gentleman to his hotel. The Stafford man, with a last hope, naively said: 'I thought I also was going into Carlton House.' 'Another mistake of yours' replied Sheridan. The worthy constituent returned that night to Stafford; and in future his vote was given against Sheridan.

Despite the precautions taken by Sheridan to preserve his investment, on the evening of 24th February 1809 the Drury Lane theatre burned down. The much-vaunted safety curtain was found to have rusted into immobility and the roof top reservoirs were empty. The catastrophe left Sheridan a ruined man. He bore the loss with fortitude and humorous resignation. At the height of the blaze, he wandered off to the Piazza coffee-house in Covent Garden where some of his friends found him and urged him to return. He smiled and said: 'Things have come to a pretty pass when a man can no longer enjoy a quiet drink in front of his own fireside'.

He never lost his sense of mischievousness or sharp wit and some weeks later encountered the Prince of Wales (later George IV) and his brother, the Duke of York, leaving the Piazza coffee-house. They were in a merry mood and the Duke, in his bluff bantering way said: 'Tell me, Sherry, for I do not know – what are you: a fool or a knave?' Taking the Prince on one arm and the Duke on the other, he replied: 'Tell the truth, sir, I am somewhat between the two'.

Another actor who ended his days without very much to show for his labours was Edwin Jehosophat Odell, a former member of Sir Henry Irving's company. For fifty years the most colourful luminary of the Savage Club, he had a sculptured face, a long bony nose, a shiny bald head, Mephistophelian eyebrows and a beard which bifurcated about three inches past the chin and terminated below his shirt collar in twin points. All this conspired to give him the look of a fearsome compound of Rasputin, Wallace Beery and The Old Man of the Sea.

When he was well past ninety and had nowhere else to go, 'Old Odell' passed his nights on one of the Club's back-room sofas. When this infringement of the rules was brought to the notice of the committee, his membership was withdrawn. He spent several days pottering about in front of the Club until a band of sympathetic fellow Savages instituted a campaign for his reinstatement. They installed him in a carriage in front of the portico, sustaining him with food smuggled from the dining room. Rather than face the old man's reproachful stares each time they crossed the threshold the members of the committee at last acknowledged that they had been outmanoeuvred and allowed him back.

In no way inhibited by a sense of gratitude, 'Old Odell' continued as rude and unpleasant as ever. He lived to be almost one hundred and never ceased to abuse other members wherever he found them. When he caught the Duke of York (later George VI) sitting in his chair, he ordered him out in language which made no concession to rank. Indeed he never considered other people at all. He once borrowed ten shillings (fifty pence) from a new and rather naive young member. When the youth had the temerity to ask for it back, half a year later, Odell snapped: 'I haven't finished with it yet'. He would be pleased to know that his chair is still preserved. It boasts a brass plate inscribed: 'Here Odell Sat'. There is no reference to King George.

Odell was by no means the only eccentric clubman of the day. At about the same period, a mere stone's-throw away at Crockford's, Lord Glasgow hurled a servant through one of the Club's windows. When the secretary attempted to remonstrate with him, he muttered: 'Put him on the bill'. A similar attack of cholera induced the Marquis of Queensbury to bite the hand that fed him by prosecuting the committee at Crockford's for serving him game beyond the close-season; and when Lord George Bentinck found himself dining in close proximity to Sir St Vincent Cotton, he peremptorily ordered the waiter to bring him the other's account. Having studied it, he coolly handed it back, saying in a loud voice: 'Before Sir St Vincent Cotton ordered so expensive a meal he ought to have paid his debts'.

Sir St Vincent Cotton never did pay his debts. Although he continued 'to *dress* like a gentleman', he ended his days as a common coachman. Having a greater command of horses than money, he proved exceptionally able. In a long career he was only ever involved in one accident which occurred on Kew Bridge while he was riding on the box as a passenger. An iron railing entered his leg. The wound was not serious.

With the exception of Sir St Vincent Cotton, few aristocrats ever learned how the 'other half' lived. Princess Charlotte said she would 'rather eat beef than starve'; and when the thirteenth Duke of Norfolk was told that some of his tenants had no food he suggested they eat curry powder. Another Victorian aristocrat was charged by his friends with being so out of touch with ordinary life that he had probably 'never even ridden on an omnibus'. He conceded that this was so and boarded the first one that came along. When the conductor said 'Where to, Guv'ner?' he said: 'A hundred and thirty-seven Eaton Square'.

The late Victorian period represented the hey-day of the eccentric. But, with the death of the Queen in 1901, the old order began to fade. It did not disappear entirely, however, or at once. There were throw-backs – the most conspicuous being Valentine Brown, Lord Castlerosse.

Although he was born fractionally too late to be a real Edwardian, Valentine personified the last of the true gentlemen eccentrics. His elbow having been shot away in the Great War, he was forced to hold his arm at a peculiar angle to his body and this, together with his considerable bulk, made him look like a stately Spanish galleon under full sail. For many years he wrote the *Londoner's Log* in the *Sunday Express*. But he never foresook his first love, which was shooting, and Lord Beaverbrook used to remark: 'If it's a fine day tomorrow, Valentine, I suppose you'll want to kill something'.

His rod-makers had their premises in St James's Street and whenever Valentine called on them an assistant was required to carry an armful of rods to the edge of the pavement so that his Lordship could make practice casts into the traffic. He had numerous rods and hardly needed more, but Valentine was an acquisitor. He took four hundred books on a ten-day sea cruise and once, on impulse, purchased at auction a lot of one hundred and forty-seven golf clubs. He was an erratic golfer but never let his performance depress him. When he got into a bunker he had a tendency to drop to his knees and pray. On one occasion, having held this position for fully three minutes, he started to rise, appeared to have second thoughts, closed his eyes again and added: 'But don't send Jesus – this is no job for a boy'.

Chapter 2

The Man Who Knew Everything

John Burdon Sanderson Haldane never ceased to be amused by the fact that he was born on Guy Fawke's Day; whether this amusement was due to his mild, if life-long attachment to pyromania, or to some other reason entirely, no one could ever discover. Some things he kept to himself and none of the Haldanes are easy to fathom.

Although they claimed to be able to trace their ancestry to Pedro the Cruel, a fourteenth century king of Castile and Leon, by the time JBS appeared on the scene in 1892, the Haldanes had transformed themselves into a respectable group of bloody-minded, ferociously intellectual Oxford academics, living in a Victorian villa at 4 St Margaret's Road. As his sister Naomi was later to record: 'it was not a God-centred household; we were brought up as highly moral agnostics'.

JBS's early life was deeply influenced by his father, John Scott Haldane, known as 'Uffa'. JS Haldane was a man almost entirely devoid of fear; and as Waynflete Professor at Oxford, his devotion to science was absolute. He detested the practice of experimenting on animals and, whenever possible, substituted human guinea-pigs. If there were no human guinea-pigs, he experimented on himself.

He also took great pains to involve his family in his work; and when asked to look into the possiblity of exterminating vermin with poison gas, took them all to France to witness the demonstration of a revolutionary new technique. The rats were loaded aboard a ship, in air-tight holds, which were then pumped full of sulphur dioxide. When the hatches were unbattened, the Haldanes amused themselves by taking it in turns to run down the ramp, their mouths tightly closed and pinching their noses, to see who could retrieve the greatest number of rats at one go without actually passing out.

If this was all good Victorian fun, it had a serious underlying purpose. Uffa was at work instilling in his children a deep respect for essential scientific principles. It is characteristic that he chose to do so not by rote, or by making them read books, but by exposing them to situations in which, if they failed to observe certain very essential rules, the consequences would be at least unpleasant and possibly very dire.

Not long after the trip to France, on a visit to a pit in north Staffordshire, JBS was exposed to another example of his father's empirical method's of education. They were crawling along one of the shafts of the pit when they encountered a patch of methane gas. The flame of Uffa's safety lamp turned blue, emitted a sharp 'pop' and went out. As soon as it did so, JBS was ordered to stand up and recite Mark Antony's speech from *Julius Caesar*. He had hardly made a start, however, before he began to feel dizzy and had to sink to the floor again. His father said: 'You have just learned an invaluable lesson: gas, being lighter than air, always rises'.

Perhaps not surprisingly, JBS displayed signs of mental precocity almost from birth. At ten months he screamed so loudly that he induced a hernia. Two years later he had learned to read. Soon after this he accidentally cut himself. He contemplated the blood and then asked his mother: 'Is that oxyhaemoglobin or carboxyhaemoglobin?' By the age of four he was leaving notes about the house reading 'I hate you'; and at the age of eight he was helping his father in his laboratory.

According to contemporary reports, Uffa needed all the help he could get. His absent-mindedness was legendary, even by Oxford standards. One night, his wife arranged a dinner-party for a number of Uffa's colleagues. On their arrival, she discovered that he had gone to bed. When she went upstairs and taxed him with this, he yawned and said: 'I suddenly found myself taking my clothes off so I thought it must be time to go to sleep'. Another time he brought home 'a plague rat from the Lister Institute in a paper bag' which he left 'in his overcoat pocket'.

Fired by a similar spirit of scientific enquiry, his son took to lying 'on the ground with maize up his shorts' in order that his pet fantail pigeons which lived in a pigeon house on top of a pole at St Margaret's Road might 'wriggle in to get it.' His mother rather frowned on this activity. With the exception of the children's macaw named Polly which used to sit on her shoulder and 'feed her ear with food pellets', she rather disapproved of pets. Polly was tolerated for her transparent kindness: if someone in the family was ill, she would regurgitate pellets of food as a sick-bed offering.

The young JBS utilised his budding knowledge to amuse his sister, Naomi, 'making the water in the basin live – off the ordinary electricity when we got it – and putting in pennies for me to snatch'. Not to be outdone, Naomi cut open one of her dolls, dribbling the contents 'into a small cauldron' which she then heated. 'I can remember my disappointment that it still wasn't edible.' She was a precocious child but, unlike her brother, still young enough to need 'areas of safety; nothing could get at me if I curled up on my father's lap, holding on to his ear with one thumb tucked into it'.

The affinity between brother and sister was strong. Both rather clumsy, when – at different periods – they overturned ink-wells at the Dragon School, they offered the identical excuse: 'Please, sir, the ink has gone and spilt itself'. When JBS fractured his skull and had to be put to bed, the house was enjoined to silence for several days. Many years after, Naomi said: 'For him, I fell all the way down a flight of steps and never squeaked'.

As soon as he was better, they resumed their boisterous games. Naomi so enjoyed these that seventy years later she confessed that she could still not go into an unfamiliar house without 'giving it a quick look-over for its hide-and-seek possibilities'.

If noise and high spirits were actively encouraged at St Margaret's Road, children were expected in other things to conform to a rigid code of Edwardian behaviour. Learning that the butler had inadvertently opened the door while Naomi was taking a bath, her mother said: 'Did he see you? If so, he must leave the house at once'.

In 1904 JBS won a scholarship to Eton, passing the entrance examination with ease. His lowest mark was seventy-eight percent. Nevertheless, he was not happy there. His brilliance caused him to be disliked and, although he was a large sturdy boy, he was subjected to a fair degree of bullying. In the course of one term he was beaten every night for a week. When his uncle – Lord Haldane of Cloan, the distinguished Queen's Counsellor and future Secretary of State at War – came to take him out to tea, JBS was prevented from seeing him: his classmates had pinioned him to the floor, beneath an upturned table, which they had then loaded with bags of sand.

These and similar incidents generated an implacable hostility towards authority in Haldane and it lasted for the rest of his life. He knew that he was different and he refused to change. Change would have been construed as a tacit admission of defeat. By the end of his time at Eton his brilliance, especially in the field of mathematics, was universally acknowledged; and when it was rumoured that he was even giving lessons to the maths master, his victory was complete.

From Eton, JBS went up to New College, Oxford. His time there served to fix his lifelong interest in genetics – although his exhaustive study of his sister's three hundred guinea-pigs appears to have baffled his tutors. Naomi had started keeping guinea-pigs some time around her twelfth birthday, after she broke her leg. She induced the first pair 'to nibble off a wart . . . on my right hand by holding it against the netting of the cage. It never came back'.

Life was not all study for JBS during these years. He possessed the usual undergraduate high spirits, loved good company and good beer and was frequently locked out. The first time this happened he spent the night under a tree in the Parks, although he might easily have gone home. The next day he devised several ingenious ways of regaining his rooms unobserved. At the end of the Great War, when he became a Fellow of the College, he had these routes 'blocked up'. Some of the undergraduates complained that this was mean-minded – which it was. JBS merely said: 'It will make you more inventive' – which it did.

In the summer of 1914, Haldane left Oxford with a Double First. He was then twenty-two. Shortly afterwards he obtained a commission in the Black Watch and was posted to France. He enjoyed the war immensely, even the killing, and during one period didn't remove his boots for three weeks, a circumstance which led General Haig to describe him as 'the bravest and dirtiest soldier in my army'.

Soon after this remark was made, JBS led his platoon into action and was knocked senseless by the blast from an enemy bomb. When he came round, he staggered to a Red Cross post and hauled himself into one of the ambulances. (Curiously, the driver was the future Edward VIII, whom Haldane had known at University.) He never had much recollection of the incident and used to pretend that only events preceeding it seemed real to him. Years afterwards, in a letter to Robert Graves, he said he thought he had entirely 'imagined events since 1915. They are now becoming rather outrageous, so perhaps I shall wake up'.

After the war, he became seriously interested in politics. Although he was ultimately to become a communist, he began as a liberal, then gravitated to socialism. At that date the Labour Party was a relatively new force. Its meetings were often disrupted by rowdy, even violent, hecklers. JBS, who weighed seventeen stone in his socks, was employed as a watchdog-cum-bouncer. The role appealed to the war-like side of his nature. But when he removed a particularly violent heckler by approaching him from behind, inserting one finger into each of his nostrils and dragging him backwards up the aisle 'like a hooked trout', even the party faithful on the platform were appalled.

When not assaulting his fellow men at political rallies, JBS now spent much of his time in his laboratory at New College, to which he had returned as a Fellow, devising ways to prolong their lives by subjecting his own body to a series of truly terrifying experiments. He drank a near-fatal dose of calcium chloride and suffered, as a result, intense diarrhoea followed by hideously painful constipation which he likened to 'a knife turning inside me'. He consumed a vast quantity of hydrochloric acid, which caused him to ride home on his bicycle like a man possessed; and to test a theory on lung capacity he ran twenty times up a flight of stairs one hundred and fifty feet high after eating an ounce and a half of bicarbonate of soda.

If JBS sometimes pushed himself to the limit in his quest for scientific knowledge, he was quite prepared to do the same to others. Nor did he always bother to obtain their consent in advance. Addressing a public meeting at Auchterarder, he explained that many of the gases used in the Great War had been manufactured to very simple formulae because their main purpose was not to kill but to incapacitate. To prove this, he vaporised a spoonful of pepper over a spirit lamp. The hall was quickly filled with pungent smoke. People began running for the doors, dabbing at their eyes and clutching at their throats. Looking after them, Haldane said: 'If that upsets you how would you like a deluge of poison gas from an air fleet in real war?'

A lesser man would have been sued. Thanks to the immensely successful series of articles which he had begun to write in the popular press – articles which explained scientific principles in non-technical terms for the benefit of the layman – he was spared this fate. He was becoming a household name and a celebrity: as such, his motives were understood and his actions forgiven. Although he relished his popular success, he remained privately contemptuous of journalists and journalism, remarking: 'The only thing you can believe in a newspaper is the date'.

In spite of this, he took the trouble to join the Rationalist Press Association and in 1925 attended one of their dinners. The guest speaker was a man named Whale. Moments after he had proposed the toast of 'eat, drink and be merry, for tomorrow we die', he dropped down dead. The appalled silence was interrupted by JBS who whispered: 'My God, the Whale's been harpooned'.

The same year, Professor Haldane left Oxford to become Reader in Biochemistry at Trinity College, Cambridge. He also undertook to do a certain amount of teaching. This delighted the students, who not only respected his considerable intellectual gifts but revelled in his idiosincracies.

His legendary inability to manipulate even the most simple piece of laboratory equipment is still remembered at Cambridge. He never attempted to conceal this, choosing rather to turn it into a joke.

Taking his female students on one side, he confided to them, in a stage whisper, that they mustn't expect him to manipulate an insect on to the glass slide of a microscope – it was simply beyond him. 'But I do claim to be an accomplished exponent of the use of the parental apparatus.'

Despite his brusqueness, JBS was a good friend to anyone younger or less influential than himself. One student, faced with a problem of epic difficulty, approached the Professor for advice. Haldane said: 'Let me think about it'. The next morning the student found the answer, represented by four closely typed sheets of paper, on his desk. The morning after that, the solution had been reduced to one page. The third morning it had been refined into an equation. Appended to this, in JBS's scrawling hand, was a note which said: 'And for the future don't ask so many damned questions'.

When a second student, Martin Case, was charged with careless driving, he mentioned this to JBS, adding that he was worried a conviction might jeopardise his career. JBS muttered: 'Leave it to me'. On the afternoon of the hearing, a crucial prosecution witness, a well-known local inebriate, turned up so drunk that he had to be supported into the witness box. His evidence was slurred and made no sense. The magistrates had no option but to dismiss the case.

It later transpired that JBS had sought the man out, earlier in the day, and plied him with whisky. Case was almost speechless with gratitude. When he did find his voice there was no stopping him. Holding up a large, hairy hand, JBS said: 'Don't be too effusive in your thanks until *this* little corollary has been adjusted' – and pulled from his pocket a tattered envelope on which he had itemised the cost of every drink. It came to a fairly steep sum but, as JBS pointed out, the man was a hardened drinker 'and I was forced to consume rather more myself that I am used to do on a weekday morning'. Case paid up. The bill was anyway a good deal less than the fine he might have expected to pay if found guilty.

In the laboratory, Professor Haldane was not always so well disposed towards his students. He detested inattention; and slovenliness in any form was liable to send him into one of his famous rages. Yet his complexity was such, it was not always possible to rely even on that. One day, conducting an experiment which involved the use of mercury, he watched in disbelief as student after student spilled or otherwise wasted the valuable substance. After the fourth spillage, Haldane lost his temper. When he recovered it, a fifth student, conducting an analysis of breath, accidentally allowed the mercury to trickle into the Professor's mouth. The class held its breath in horrified anticipation. Haldane, realising perhaps that his display of temperament had contributed to the boy's nervousness, merely spat it out and said: 'I am not syphilitic yet'.

This ambivalent attitude to people and events occasionally manifested itself as a contradictory blend of generosity and suspicion. He was always ready to lend books to his students but never failed, before doing so, to write on the inside cover: 'This book belongs to J. B. S. Haldane'.

In the summer of 1924 Haldane met Charlotte Burghes, the lady who was to become his first wife. Charlotte was a journalist and married. It soon became evident that a divorce would have to be obtained. In order for this to stand up in court it had to be proven that one or other of the partners had committed adultery. Haldane approached the Vice-Chancellor of the University and in his typically forthright manner 'told him that I was about to commit this act, to which he replied "Oh!"'

JBS and Charlotte arranged to be followed to their hotel by a detective employed by Charlotte's husband. Unfortunately, Charlotte took an instant dislike to the place and insisted they find another. JBS was against this, reasoning that the detective would never find them. Using her feminine intuition, Charlotte went down to the foyer, sniffed the man out and enlisted his help in transferring their lugguage. The next morning, absolutely on cue and accompanied by the required number of corroborative witnesses, he burst into their room, thoughtfully bringing their morning newspaper with him, and 'caught' them.

In due course the divorce went through. But the matter did not end there. Under the statutes of the University, its moral guardian, the Sex Viri ('which' said Haldane 'means the Six Men not the Sex Weary') was empowered to remove from his post any Reader who was guilty of 'gross or habitual immorality'. The Sex Viri so found and Haldane was deprived of his Readership. He eventually retrieved it, but not without a battle and a series of tiresome, protracted and much publicised appeals.

He never forgave the University. But for the present it suited his purpose to remain. Life returned to normal. He rode to work each day on his antiquated bone-shaker of a bicycle wearing, even in winter, a shirt open at the neck. In summer he took himself off to a local pool where, utterly naked and like some benign walrus, he executed a sedate breast stroke, puffing on his pipe as he swam.

Although his relationship with Charlotte was eventually to sour – possibly because despite his 'accomplished use of the parental apparatus' he was unable to father a child – they were at first very happy. In the evenings, Charlotte wrote and JBS trained the family cat to sit on the top of the door and launch itself on to the shoulders of unsuspecting visitors. He was hopelessly attached to this cat, as he was to all God's creatures. He once said: 'I have been a research scientist for thirty years. I have never wittingly inflicted pain on any animal'. Even the cobwebs in his study were left undisturbed for fear of rendering the spiders homeless. When visitors taxed him with this, he would cite Thomas Day, the romantic idealist and disciple of Rousseau. One afternoon a lawyer companion asked Day to crush a spider that was annoying him. He refused, saying: 'Let us suppose that some superior being should say to a companion "Kill that lawyer", how should you like it? And a lawyer is more noxious to most people than a spider'.

In 1932, JBS relinquished his Cambridge Readership and moved to University College London. He remained there for the best part of a quarter of a century, devoting much of that time to an exclusive study of genetics. For thirteen years – an ominous number – life was uneventful. But in 1945 Charlotte petitioned for a divorce. As soon as this was made absolute, JBS married his research assistant, Dr Helen Spurway.

There were those at the time who condemned Charlotte's decision to end the marriage, but JBS was not the easiest of men with whom to live. The continuous experiments to which he had subjected himself over the years had played havoc with his metabolism and this had tended to increase his irascibility. He could be appallingly quarrelsome and difficult. When he was asked to participate in a programme with three eminent colleagues, the BBC felt it necessary 'to take special precautions against possible murder by having each of the four contributors record their contributions' separately – that is, 'under circumstances which ensured against their meeting on the stairs'.

It was a wise decision: JBS was notorious for being rude to people. On one ocasion, pottering about the library at University College and being unable to locate a book he required, he approached the librarian for assistance. She told him the volume was not in stock. Thrusting out his chin – and it was a very formidable chin – he said: "I bet you £50 you're wrong" and commanded her to go and look. In fact, it was

JBS who was wrong. He compounded the offence by insisting on writing her a cheque in settlement of the bet. By the time he had done so, the poor girl had been reduced to tears.

His response to things for which he could discover no rational – that is, *scientific* – explanation was equally aggressive. Asked whether he believed in extrasensory perception, he said: 'I suppose so – but it's still a damned invasion of one's privacy'; and when he walked into his study and encountered his *alter ego* sitting in *his* chair and smoking *his* pipe, he simply walked across the room and sat on it. He was equally decisive when it came to voicing opinions. He believed that 'No Perfume' compartments on the railways would have benefited passengers far more than 'No Smoking' ones; and when he was presented with the motion that 'This House believes in Western Democracy' by a student debating society, he said: 'I am not prepared to support a motion so carelessly framed. I do not know what it means. It reminds me of the aged don at Cambridge who was heard to say in chapel "And I believe in Pontius Pilate – oh, no I don't"'.

During the Second World War, Haldane carried out vital research into underwater warfare for the Admiralty which later culminated in the successful attack on the *Tirpitz*. A second project involved exploring advanced techniques of underwater breathing. This eventually saved the lives of countless seamen trapped in torpedo-damaged submarines – but it was highly dangerous work.

In order to bring it to fruition, JBS and Martin Case (the careless driver of his Cambridge days) spent endless hours locked in a pressure chamber from which the air was then slowly extracted. Both men noted down their reactions to this process with meticulous care until they were either rendered unconscious or were seen to be in such physical distress that the pressure chamber had to be stabilised. As stabilisation had often to be carried out very swiftly, both men suffered habitual and acute attacks of convulsions, oxygen poisoning and quite dreadful nose bleeds. It became something of a standing joke that anyone wishing to locate them had only to follow the trail of blood-stained wads of cotton wool which they dropped behind them wherever they went. Although he was careful never to admit as much to his colleagues, JBS was privately convinced that the experiments would kill him. He was no longer a young man, nor was he in the best of condition.

After the war, JBS returned to the life of a research scientist at University College. He was constantly at loggerheads with the administrators – anaemic bureaucrats devised by Satan to keep him short of money and thereby impede the smooth running of his department – and when, in 1957, he was offered a post with the Indian Statistical Institute, he accepted it with relief. To the press – 'never believe anything you read in a newspaper but the date' – he variously rationalised his decision to leave England as a protest at the 'outrageous' intervention in Suez by British troops the year before, and as a heaven-sent opportunity to leave off 'wearing socks. Sixty years of socks is enough'. In fact, he and Helen had been interested in the Indian way of life for years.

The administrators were no doubt glad to see the back of him. Not so his students. One of them probably spoke for many when he said: 'I felt that in Professor Haldane I had found the one man who might just know everything there is to be known'.

In India – in some respects the most callous of God's continents – Haldane continued to demonstrate his love for the small and defenceless creatures of this world. One day he discovered an injured bird, took it home and operated on it. He then sent to England to learn how best to fashion it a false wing-tip. He was careful to apply a little pressure by adding that if English technology couldn't supply the answer he would get 'someone from the local Indian Air Force Medical service on to the job'. He had high hopes of getting it airborne again. 'If I succeed, it will be called Bader.'

In 1961 he was made an honorary Fellow of New College. This delighted Naomi who reminded him that he could now go into areas of that hallowed institution where, as children, they had only dared trespass. 'Ah,' said Haldane 'but now we are ghosts.' It was the remark of a very tired man.

Four years later, at the age of seventy-nine, and whilst on a lecture tour of the United States, Haldane noticed signs of anal bleeding. Although he suspected a rectal carcinoma, he refused to enter hospital for tests. He would not let down 'the many people who have paid good money to hear me speak'.

Once the tour was over, however, he was admitted to University College Hospital at once. The cancer – although not at first its malignancy – was confirmed. The BBC, with appalling bad taste but a firm knowledge of their man, asked him to make a filmed obituary. He said: 'a goodbye to all that from a hospital bed would be an excellent idea'.

He began by saying that he hoped nobody would see the film until at least 1975 'when I shall be eighty-two years old, which is perhaps old enough. However, I have just been operated on for cancer and if the operation is not a success you will be seeing and hearing me a lot sooner'. At this point the producer noticed that he was doodling on the blotter which had been placed in front of him. When the camera attempted to focus on this, he obscured it with his hand. Trying to get him to reveal what he had written, the producer said: 'Don't worry, it will probably be all Greek to most people'. Haldane smiled mischievously and retorted: 'It *is* Greek and maybe it's Greek to you – but it's still obscene to those who understand it'.

Before he left London for the last time, JBS wrote from his hospital bed a poem entitled *Cancer's a Funny Thing*. It confirmed his opinion that it is impossible to write anything without offending someone and it earned him praise and censure in almost equal measure. It is nonetheless a remarkable piece of work:

> I wish I had the voice of Homer
> To sing of rectal carcinoma

Which kills a lot more chaps, in fact,
Than were bumped off when Troy was sacked.
I noticed I was passing blood
(Only a few drops, not a flood)
So pausing on my homeward way
From Tallahassee to Bombay
I asked a doctor, now my friend,
To peer into my hinder end,
To prove or to disprove the rumour
That I had a malignant tumour.
They pumped in BA SO4
Till I could really stand no more,
And when sufficient had been pressed in,
They photographed my large intestine
In order to decide the issue
They next scraped out some bits of tissue.
(Before they did so, some good pal
Had knocked me out with pentothal,
Whose action is extremely quick,
And does not leave me feeling sick.)
The microscope returned the answer
That I had certainly got cancer
So I was wheeled into the theatre
Where holes were made to make me better
One set is in my perineum
Where I can feel but can't yet see 'em.
Another made me like a kipper
Or female prey of Jack the Ripper.
Through this incision, I don't doubt,
The Neoplasm was taken out,
Along with colon and lymph nodes
Where cancer cells might find abodes.
A third much smaller hole is meant
To function as a ventral vent:
So now I am like two-faced Janus
The only God who sees his anus
I'll swear without the risk of perjury,
It was a snappy bit of surgery.
My rectum is a serious loss to me,
But I've a very neat colostomy,
And hope, as soon as I am able,

To make it keep a fixed time-table.
So do not wait for aches and pains
To have a surgeon mend your drains:
If he says 'Cancer' you're a dunce
Unless you have it out at once,
For if you wait it's sure to swell
And may have progeny as well.
My final word before I'm done
Is 'Cancer Can Be Rather Fun'.
Thanks to the nurses and Nye Bevan
The National Health is quite like heaven
Provided one confronts the tumour
With a sufficient sense of humour.
I know that cancer often kills,
But so do cars and sleeping-pills;
And it can hurt one till one sweats,
But so can bad teeth and unpaid debts.
A spot of laughter, I am sure,
Often accelerates one's cure;
So let us patients do our bit
To help the surgeons make us fit.

Despite the poem's rather jaunty tone, JBS was dying. His wife was aware of this before they left London for home. For some inexplicable reason the surgeons had chosen not to tell their patient. When he discovered the truth, he wrote to the hospital to complain – not on his own behalf, but for those he would leave behind. He said: 'The result . . . of concealment has been disastrous. I have been making rather elaborate plans for the future and several young men will be let down. Why cannot people learn to speak the truth? I have, I think, taught two, perhaps three Indian colleagues to do so – it will probably wreck their careers'.

A few weeks later, John Burdon Sanderson Haldane was resting quietly on the verandah of his Indian home when his condition suddenly worsened. Before the doctors could reach him, his wish to die 'preferably on an easy chair . . . on my verandah, looking at flowering trees and birds in the sunshine' had been granted. A scientist to the last, he left his body to medical research, stressing that 'its refrigeration . . . should be a first charge on my estate'.

Chapter 3

Brollies, Bowlers and Builders

In the eighteenth and nineteenth centuries, as England's power and influence increased, a new type of eccentric began to emerge. Sometimes aristocratic, invariably wealthy, he was distinguished from other eccentrics by his deep mistrust of his fellow man and by a love of secrecy which often bordered on the manic. The first of these was 'the Master of Fonthill', William Beckford, born in 1760 the son of William Beckford, a rich West India merchant who was twice Lord Mayor of London. William Beckford senior was the outspoken defender of freedom who in 1770 supported John Wilkes by embroidering the front of his house in Soho Square with the word 'Liberty' in white letters three feet high. 'Luckily' says Horace Walpole 'the evening was very wet and not a mouse stirred.'

When Lord Mayor Beckford died, in June 1770, he left his ten-year-old son a fortune of a million pounds and an income of a hundred thousand pounds a year. Despite the softening influence of the young Mozart – who gave him music lessons – William Beckford junior was a difficult child who grew into an extravagant, withdrawn and temperamental young man. He was in youth a great traveller and completed the Grand Tour before his twentieth year. Being rich, he was able to do so in style and is said never to have travelled anywhere without his own bed.

Before discovering his true career as an eccentric builder, he frequently amused himself by sending for his Steward and ordering a vast meal for a dozen guests. But when the table was laid and the footmen positioned behind the chairs, he would sit down alone, taste one dish and retire to bed.

At the age of twenty-one, Beckford produced *Vathek*, a highly imaginative Gothic novel which revealed in its style the influence of Voltaire, with whom he enjoyed a close friendship. 'It took me,' he was to recall in old age, 'three days and two nights of hard labour. I never took off my clothes the whole time. This severe application made me very ill.'

Nine years after its publication, he retired to the village of his birth, Fonthill in Wiltshire, where some years earlier his father had purchased a large estate and erected a grand mansion which in 1755 burned down. When William Beckford senior was informed of this catastrophe he sat down, took out his pocket book and began making notes. When someone asked what he was doing, he said he was calculating the cost of rebuilding it. 'It won't be above a thousand pounds each to my [natural] children and I have an odd fifty thousand pounds in a drawer.'

In due course, this house passed to his son. Being of a different generation, the younger Beckford disliked it. It stood 'too near a piece of water', which he thought might induce rheumatism or the ague. In consequence it was mostly taken down and in 1802 the furniture of the Turkish Room, which had cost his father more than four thousand pounds was sold at auction for just seven hundred and forty guineas.

Beckford now decided to indulge his new-found passion for building by erecting a third house on the site, a showy, monastic structure which he christened Fonthill Abbey. Having first constructed a new hamlet to accommodate them, he hired a regiment of artisans to labour round the clock, working at night by the light of torches. Their employer's enthusiasm was such that anything conceived had to be put into effect immediately. The workmen were kept literally supplied with drink and when anything was completed which gave the master particular pleasure he paid bonuses of five or ten shillings a man, money which was also spent on drink.

The house took eighteen years to complete and cost £273,000. Its crowning glory was a central tower two hundred and seventy-six feet high, rivalling in grace and loftiness the spire of Salisbury Cathedral, a few miles away. Unfortunately, in order to placate William's obsession with speed, the work had to be skimped and the tower collapsed. Nothing daunted, William had his drunken workmen rebuild it.

Believing that nothing was impossible to a man of means, he 'swore by his beloved St Anthony that he would have his Christmas dinner cooked in the new Abbey kitchen'. According to John Timbs:

> Time was short, the work was severe, for much remained to be done. Still, Beckford had said it, and it must be done. So every exertion that money could command was brought to bear. The apartment, indeed, was finished by the Christmas morning, but the bricks had not time to settle readily into their places, the beams were not thoroughly secured, the mortar, which was to keep the walls together, had not dried. However, Beckford had invoked the blessed St Anthony, and he would not depart from it. The fire was lit, the splendid repast was cooked, the servants were carrying the dishes through the long passages into the dining-room, when the kitchen itself fell in with a loud crash. But it was not a misfortune of any consequence; no person was injured, the master had kept his word, and he had money enough to build another kitchen.

By the autumn of 1800 the mansion was partially completed and in the December, Lord Nelson and Sir William and Lady Hamilton were entertained here in regal splendour. On their departure, Beckford installed his bizarre retinue in their suite: three dogs (known respectively as Caroline, Nephew and Viscount Fartlebury), an Italian dwarf who ate nothing but mushrooms and a group of homosexual servants on whom he bestowed grotesque nicknames such as 'the Doll' and 'the Calf'.

In order to protect his privacy, the estate was bounded by a wall seven miles long, twelve feet high and topped by sharp spikes. the gate lodge was permanently guarded. He seldom ventured beyond the boundaries of his estate because, says Timbs:

> he was generally asked for charity by the poor people. Sometimes he used to throw a one-pound note or a guinea to them; or he would turn round and give the supplicants a severe horse-whipping. When the last was the case, soon after he had ridden

away, he generally sent back a guinea or two to the persons whom he had whipped.

Beckford lived at Fonthill in reclusive splendour. Occasionally, in the half-light which exists shortly before dawn, a figure was glimpsed galloping across the park, riding as if pursued by ten thousand devils and lashing his horse to a lather. Just as it seemed that the animal must drop dead, the rider would rein to a halt and fling himself fully clothed into the cold green lake.

Only one man ever succeeded in breaching the security at Fonthill, a relative of the artist, W. P. Frith.* He did so for a bet – and to see the gardens, which were said to be the finest in the West. He slipped in while the lodge keeper was occupied with a tradesman. He had not been long about his business when he was challenged by a 'shabby fellow holding a potato'. Frith's relative confessed that he was a trespasser, but added that his only desire had been to view the gardens. He was turning to go when, with some diffidence, his companion offered to show him round. Having done so – and much to the trespasser's surprise – he offered to show him the house.

The first thing which impressed itself on the visitor was the scale, the sheer vastness of the building. From the southern end of the mansion he had an unobstructed view stretching away three hundred feet to the northern wall. Each of the rooms contained a host of treasures, 'the viewing of which left me quite surfeited'. At the end of

* Frith vouched for the truth of the story in his autobiography.

the tour, the 'gardener' revealed that he was William Beckford and invited his visitor to stay to dinner.

Throughout the splendid meal, which was washed down by excellent wines, Beckford kept up a dazzling monologue on a variety of subjects. His guest, however, was hardly listening: he was mulling over the tale he would have to tell his friends.

Some time before midnight, 'the Master of Fonthill' rose from the table and excused himself. His companion, thinking that he had some private business to conduct, made himself comfortable against his return. But Beckford did not return.

Frith's relative was woken from a fitful doze by one of the footmen. The man announced that his master had retired for the night and, leading the unfortunate dupe to the door, said: 'Mr Beckford orders me to present his compliments to you sir, and I am to say that as you found your way into Fonthill Abbey without assistance, you may find your way out again as best you can; and he hopes you will take care to avoid the bloodhounds that are let loose in the park each night. I wish you good evening. No, thank you, sir: Mr Beckford never allows vails'.

The poor man was forced to climb into the nearest tree where he sat it out until break of day. He had won his wager, but as he later admitted to his friends: 'Not for fifty million times the amount would I again pass such a night as I did at Fonthill Abbey'.

Beckford's fortunes ultimately suffered a sharp decline when the Court of Chancery deprived him of two of his Jamaican estates. He told an acquaintance: 'You may imagine their importance when I tell you that there were fifteen hundred slaves upon them'. The property at Fonthill was placed on the market and Mr Christie instructed to prepare a catalogue for the sale of the effects. Despite the tickets of admission being priced at a guinea, more than seven thousand people flocked to view its treasures.

Although the Abbey had long been reckoned a *Folly*, it was eventually sold to a retired India merchant named Farquhar for £330,000. Two years later the tower again collapsed, thus pointing the moral that 'when the forts of folly fall' the greatest folly is to be left holding the deeds. Because they had been laid over a small summer-house – to which Beckford had been making additions when the idea of the Abbey had first occurred to him – the foundations of the tower had long been suspect. Impatient to realise the scheme: 'he would not wait to remove the summer-house to make a proper foundation . . . but carried it up on the walls already standing, and this with the worst description of materials and workmanship, while it was mostly built by men in a state of intoxication'.

Of this second collapse, John Timbs records that:

> from the lightness of the materials of which it was constructed, neither Mr Farquhar, nor the servants who were in the kitchen preparing dinner, knew that it had fallen . . . [although] 'the cloud of dust was enormous, so as to completely darken the air for a considerable distance around for several minutes. Such was the concussion in the interior of the building, that one man was forced along a passage as if he had been in an air-gun to the distance of thirty feet . . . Mr Beckford, when told . . . by his servant that the tower had fallen, merely observed that it had made an obeisance to Mr Farquhar which it had never done to him.

With his circumstances so cruelly reduced, Beckford purchased two houses in Lansdown Crescent, Bath, where he recreated the splendour and state of Fonthill on a smaller scale. He united them with a magnificent flying gallery; created a series of gardens, hot-houses and conservatories; and stocked his wine cellar with nineteen pipes of fine Malmsey Madeira laid down by his father. The *Fonthill Croesus* had purchased these half a century before. The importer had originally offered them to the Queen but the price had been so high that she had not been able to afford more than one.

He continued to lead the life of a gentleman, rising early and always taking a walk before breakfast. He read until noon, 'generally making pencil notes in the margin of every book'. After transacting necessary business with his steward, he would return to his books until late afternoon when he would 'ride out two or three hours'. In 1835, at the age of seventy-five, he said that he had never felt a moment's *ennui* in his life. And when Cyrus Redding said: 'It must have cost you much pain to quit Fonthill', he smiled and said: 'Not so much as you might think. I can bend to fortune. I have philosophy enough not to cry like a child about a plaything'.

Some years prior to his death, Beckford had constructed a lofty tower at Lansdown 'to be the place of his sepulchre'. He left instructions that his body was to be placed in a granite sarcophagus inscribed with a passage from *Vathek*. The authorities refused permission and his embalmed body was interred at Lyncomb. It was moved to its present site, a table-tomb of red granite close to the Lansdown tower when the ground was properly consecrated in the late 1840s.

It has been said of William Beckford that 'he was the victim of riches' and that 'at every stage his money was like a millstone around his neck.' He was not without refinement or taste, but he was extravagant, whimsical and a slave to instant gratification. As John Timbs has sensibly pointed out: 'Had he only had five thousand a year, and been sent to Eton, he might have been one of the foremost men of his time'. In the end 'he was the worst: for he so threw about his money at Fonthill as to corrupt and demoralise the simple country people'.

'Against this judgement must, however, be placed [his] own declaration that he never felt a single moment of *ennui*' – and that he never permitted his servants to accept vails.

The practice of giving vails, or tips – itself a highly eccentric custom – was then very widespread. In furtherance of being paid twice over, servants tyrannised both their employers and their employers' guests to a degree which now seems hardly credible. Everybody expected to receive something and upper servants expected to receive a great deal. If this failed to live up to their expectations they sometimes became unpleasant. On one occasion, after dining with the Duke of Newcastle, Sir Timothy Waldo paused en route to his carriage to press a crown into the hand of the cook. The cook disdainfully returned it, saying: 'Sir, I do not take silver'. 'Do you not, indeed' replied Sir Timothy. 'And I do not give gold.'

By the middle of the eighteenth century tipping had become so widespread that even the rich tended to decline invitations rather than be put to the expense of maintaining other people's servants. A household such as Beckford's was very much the exception; and when a man named Cole, visiting the house of the painter William Hogarth, had his tip refused by the servant he concluded: 'This was so uncommon and so liberal in a man of Hogarth's profession at that time of day, that it much struck me, as nothing of the kind had happened to me before'.

Hogarth's reluctance to embarrass his guests may have stemmed from a sense of fellow feeling. Even after he had grown prosperous, he was often heard to say: 'I can remember the time when I have gone moping into the city without a shilling in my pocket'. By the late 1720s he had risen to become a painter of portraits – a most 'ill-suited employment for a man' who refused to flatter and could hardly 'look on vanity without a sneer'. He preferred sitting in the coffee-houses of Covent Garden, surreptitiously capturing the likeness of the patrons on his thumbnail with his pencil. His general irascibility earned him many enemies and he could be particularly forthright with those who grudged him his fees. Having indicated that 'no great price would be given for the performance', one rich nobleman commissioned him to paint a mural depicting 'Pharoah and his host drowned in the Red Sea'. Hogarth simply covered the entire area with red paint. When his patron objected, Hogarth said: 'The red, you perceive, is the Red Sea. Pharoah and his host are drowned, as you desired. They cannot be made objects of sight because the sea covers them all'.

Apart from the expense, the practice of tipping was frowned upon for lessening a servant's respect for his betters. In one aristocratic household, where the custom was widespread, the Duke one day asked his valet how the servants whiled away the hours when not on duty. The man said: 'Well, your Grace, one of our favourite amusements is piecing together the letters found in the wastepaper basket in the morning – better than any jigsaw puzzle, I can assure your Grace, and much more entertaining'.

Tipping's most implacable opponent was the eccentric merchant and traveller, Jonas Hanway. But then Hanway was 'agin' a great many things. He detested tea – which he believed to be a social evil leading to adultery, divorce and suicide; and he urged people to drink ground-ivy instead. In a long career, he wrote seventy-four books and is generally credited with having been the inventor of the umbrella, an idea suggested to him by the portable sunshades of the East. Ceremonial sunshades had been used by the ancient Egyptians and Assyrians; and the King of Burma was known to his subjects as 'The Lord of the Great Parasol'. This was a circular white canopy exclusive to the monarch. Anyone trying to steal it was put to death.

The umbrella began to gain popularity in England about 1780. At that date, acorns were sometimes attached to the handles to propitiate the god of thunder, to whom they were sacred. There were numerous teething troubles and in 1786, when it was suggested that they tended to attract lightning, a Frenchman actually went so far as to attach a conductor to the tip and walked about on rainy days with a long wire trailing behind him, acting as an earth.

Hanway's claim to be 'the Father of the Umbrella' was discredited by Bergen Evans in 'The Natural History of Nonsense.' Umbrellas, he said 'had been in general use . . . long before Jonas Hanway was born, and for anything we know those who carried them were regarded then as they are now – with envy when it was raining and contempt when it was not'.

A second millionaire misanthropist who rivalled Beckford in the scale of his building was William Cavendish-Bentinck-Scott, fifth Duke of Portland. Far beneath his country seat of Welbeck Abbey he constructed an enormous ballroom lit by a thousand gas-jets; a stable for thirty horses; and a carriage drive which gave access to the local railway station. On his infrequent visits to London – where he lived in a house surrounded by a high wall – he travelled along this subterranean route in a closely shuttered coach. Having reached the station, his carriage was loaded on to a flat-car for the journey to town.

He was equally secretive when it came to journeys on foot and went out only at night, preceeded by a woman equipped with a lantern. She had strict instructions to keep exactly fifty paces in front and never, on pain of dismissal, to look round. His Grace could not abide to look upon a human face and any servant who encountered him about the corridors of Welbeck was peremptorily ordered to go and skate on the subterranean rink.

The Duke was deeply attached to gadgetry and in this has found a spiritual successor in the former racing driver, Stirling Moss. In the mid-1970s Mr Moss owned a house in Mayfair almost entirely run by gadgets. The glass of the ground-floor windows was of the type which enables the occupant to look out whilst thwarting the attempts of the curious to gaze in. The toilet seat was kept permanently heated to body temperature and the bath could be run by remote control from either the study or the dining room. Beyond the study an interior courtyard contained a fountain, floodlit by a photo-electric cell which reacted automatically to any marked diminution in natural light. At the press of a button, a meal could be lowered on a small table from the kitchen in just eight seconds.

However, too great a reliance on mechanical aides can sometimes have unfortunate consequences – as the Scottish folklorist, Sir James Frazer, discovered to his cost. Having installed a dividing wall in his home, which could be raised or lowered at will between the ground and upper floors, he invited two married couples to stay. He put them, together, into one large top floor room which he then divided with the moveable partition. The same night, having forgotten about his visitors, he summoned the wall to eliminate a draught in his own apartment and in consequence saw nothing of his guests on the following day until nearly tea-time.

Sir James had the reputation of being a sparse eater. Equally austere in his diet was the novelist, Ronald Firbank. Something of an 'exquisite', he often astonished polite society by eating nothing for dinner but a pea. The day the proprietor of his favourite restaurant was able to persuade him to supplement this with a slice of toast was a day of general rejoicing. Unlike many eccentrics, he rather liked his fellow man and once said that 'to behold the Englishman at his *best*, one should watch him play tip-and-run'.

A third writer with eccentric eating habits was Lord Byron, a friend of 'the banker-poet' Samuel Rogers. The first time the two men sat down together, at Rogers' house in St James's Place, they were but slightly acquainted and Rogers, with great politeness, asked Byron whether:

> he would take soup? 'No; he never took soup.' – Would he take some fish? 'No; he never took fish.' – Presently I asked if he would eat some mutton. 'No; he never ate mutton.' – I then asked if he would take a glass of wine. 'No; he never tasted wine.' – It was now necessary to enquire what he *did* eat and drink; and the answer was 'Nothing but hard biscuits and soda-water'. Unfortunately, neither hard biscuits nor soda-water were at hand; and he dined upon potatoes bruised down on his plate and drenched with vinegar . . . Some days after, meeting Hobhouse, I said to him, 'How long will Lord Byron persevere in his present diet?' He replied: 'Just as long as you continue to notice it'. – I did not then know, what I now know to be a fact – that Byron, after leaving my house, had gone to a club in St James's Street and eaten a hearty meat-supper.

Byron was very wrong to pull Rogers' leg in this manner. But then Rogers was not entirely free of pretension himself. He was a laborious painstaking man whose poem 'Italy' was fifteen years in the writing. His 'Colombus' took only one year less. Sydney Smith pretended to be astonished by this and remarked:

> When Rogers produces a couplet, he goes to bed, and the knocker is tied up, and straw is laid down, and the caudle* is made and the answer to enquiries is that Mr Rogers is as well as can be expected.

Nonetheless, he was not a bad poet. Two of his lines – 'not dead but gone before' and 'to know her was to love her' – have passed into common usage. That he could be pungent as well as sentimental is demonstrated by his epigrams. 'It doesn't much signify whom one marries' said he. 'For one is sure to find next morning it was someone else.' A lifelong bachelor, Rogers was a professional host whose home over the years became:

> the envied resort of wit, beauty, learning and genius. There, surrounded by the choicest treasures of art, and in the light reflected from Guidos and Titians . . . mingled in familiar converse the most eminent poets, painters, actors, artists, critics, travellers, historians, warriors, orators and statesmen of two generations.

For all this, Thomas Carlyle found Samuel Rogers physically repulsive. He described him as 'a half-frozen Whig gentleman! no hair at all, but one of the whitest bald scalps, blue eyes shrewd, sad and cruel; toothless horse-shoe mouth drawn up to the very nose; slow-croaking, sarcastic insight, perfect breeding'. According to Benjamin Robert Haydon: 'Rogers of an evening always gave me the idea that he had been laid in a nasty place for a month and washed for the occasion. To see him standing behind a beauty was no joke'.

This was so. But it was the jokes he made that redeemed him. After viewing Haydon's picture 'Christ Blessing the Little Children', he turned to the artist and said in a very droll manner: 'When all the figures in the picture get up to walk away, I beg leave to secure the little girl in the foreground'.

If he was secretly flattered by the attention which his verses engendered, he always maintained an outward air of weariness at the

* A spiced warm drink given to the sick.

tiresome consequences of fame. This sometimes left him vulnerable. When they met by chance at a European watering spa, he confided to Lord Dudley: 'At dinner the other night I had no sooner taken my seat when the lady on my left began: "Why, I feel sure you must be Mr Rogers."' 'Indeed' said Lord Dudley. 'And *were* you?'

After their initial 'misunderstanding', Lord Byron 'used often to sup' with Rogers at St James' Place, 'but as he could not endure to see women eat . . . would write me a note to enquire if I had invited any'. Like so many of his Lordship's eccentricities, this great misogyny proved as great a humbug. Gronow confirms that the poet's chief objection to having ladies at table stemmed not:

> from a wish to believe, if possible, in their more ethereal nature . . . but from the fact of their being helped first, and consequently getting all the wings of the chicken, whilst men had to be content with the legs or other parts.

Another literary fellow 'who used often to sup' with Rogers and who shared his 'disagreeable negligence' in the matter of dress was the epic inebriate, Richard Porson. He invariably wore 'a large patch of coarse brown paper on his nose' to cover some semi-erupted pustule and his rusty black coat was hung with cobwebs. He possessed immense physical strength, high animal spirits and once, for a wager, carried a young woman around his Temple chambers in his teeth. He seldom went to bed before dawn and:

> when the evening grew late, the Fellows of Trinity used to walk out of the common room and leave Porson to himself, who was sometimes found smoking by the servants next morning, without having apparently moved from the spot where he had been left overnight.

His insomnia ultimately reduced his friends to a state of near collapse and from a sense of self-preservation it was agreed 'that he was always to go away at eleven'. He readily concurred 'but would never stir before and warmly resented any attempt to make him'.

One night he was invited to dine with Horne Tooke at Richmond Buildings. Tooke knew that 'Professor Porson *had not been in bed for the three preceding nights*' and reasonably 'expected to get rid of him at an early hour'. He had miscalculated. Porson 'kept Tooke up the whole night; and in the morning, the latter, in perfect despair, said: "Mr Porson, I am engaged to meet a friend at breakfast at a coffee-house in Leicester Square." "Oh", replied Porson. "I will go with you"; and he accordingly did so. Soon after they had reached the coffee-house, Tooke contrived to slip out, and running home, ordered his servant not to let Mr Porson in even if he should attempt to batter down the door. "A man", observed Tooke, "who could sit up four nights successively, could sit up forty."'

It was true. Porson could 'drink all night and spout all day' – if he had a mind to. But he hated being lionised and when Rogers took him to a party 'where several women of fashion desired to hear him talk', he lectured them so oddly 'on the subject of *soup*' that most of them were frightened off. The embarrassed Rogers hurried him away and left him in Piccadilly, being epically sick. The two men nonetheless continued on good terms and the Professor was a regular guest at St James' Place. He only once declined his friend's hospitality: 'the banker-poet' inviting him to dine, he answered in an off-hand sort of way: 'Thank you, no, I dined yesterday'.

Porson's eating habits were almost as bizarre as those of Lord Byron. 'At breakfast he frequently ate bread and cheese: and he then took his porter as copiously as Johnson took his tea. At Eton, he once kept Mrs Goodall at the breakfast-table during the whole of Sunday morning.'

On another occasion, he was required to go to Oxford to collate a manuscript. As the work looked likely to occupy several days, Doctor Routh, 'the president of Magdalen, who was leaving home for the long vacation, said to him at his departure, "Make my house your home, Mr Porson, for my servants have orders to be quite at your command and to procure you whatever you please." When he returned, he asked for the account of what the Professor had had during his stay. The servant brought the bill and the Doctor, glancing at it, observed a fowl entered into it for every day. "What", said he, "did you provide for Mr Porson no better than this, but oblige him to dine every day on fowl?" "No, sir", replied the servant; "but we asked the gentleman the first day what he would have for dinner, and as he did not seem to know very well what to order, we suggested a fowl. When we went to him about dinner any day afterwards, he always said: 'the same as yesterday'; and this was the only answer we could get from him."'

His taste in liquor was equally indiscriminate. On one occasion he drank a bottle of embrocation; and on another spirits for the lamp in mistake for gin. In consequence, he was a poor neighbour. One night, Baron Gurney, who for a time occupied chambers beneath Porson's in Essex Court was:

> awakened by a tremendous thump upon the floor overhead. Porson, it turned out, had come home drunk, and had tumbled down in his room, and put out his candle; for Gurney soon after heard him fumbling at the staircase lamp, and cursing the nature of things which made him see two flames instead of one.

Porson's early life had been one of poverty. In consequence 'he used often to lie awake at night praying for a large pearl'. Unfortunately, 'two Mordecais sat at his gate – thirst and procrastination', and when he did achieve some small success he found himself ill-fitted to cope with it. As he also possessed a satirical biting wit, he often alienated those who might otherwise have been his friends. One scholar, who found him insufferable, said: 'Dr Porson, my opinion of you is most contemptible'. Porson replied: 'I never knew an opinion of yours that was not contemptible'. At a dinner party, when a man asked him: 'Pray, was Captain Cook killed on his first voyage?', the Professor replied: 'I believe he was – though he did not mind it much and immediately entered on a second.'

He relished all forms of literary dispute and one day, travelling in a coach, encountered a young Oxford undergraduate who attempted to impress two young ladies with what he represented as a quotation from Sophocles. Porson, who until then had been half asleep, instantly roused himself and pounced upon him with his 'terrible memory.' 'You favoured us just now' said he 'with a quotation from Sophocles. I do not happen to recollect it.' Colouring up, the lad assured him that it was 'word for word as I have repeated it; but I suspect, sir, it is some time since you were at College'. At this, Porson rummaged about in his coat, produced a pocket edition of Sophocles and challenged him to find it. After a certain amount of fruitless endeavour, the blustering undergraduate said: 'On second thoughts, I now recollect that the passage is in *Euripides*'. Porson rummaged once more and came up with an edition of *Euripides*. 'Perhaps' said he 'you will be so good as to find it for me in *that* little book.'

Muttering: 'Curse me if I ever quote Greek again in a coach', he studied it for a moment or two and then announced: 'Bless me, sir, how dull I am: I recollect now – yes, yes, I perfectly remember that the passage is in Aeschylus'. Seeing the Doctor reaching once more into his coat, he shouted up: 'Coachman, let me out – there's a fellow here got the Bodleian library in his pocket. He must be Porson – or the devil!'

Another odd and curious literary giant who – if we are to believe Stephen Hawker – 'yielded to the conqueror of Ariadne ever and anon' was Alfred Lord Tennyson. But unlike Rogers or Byron or Porson, there was something in his personality which seems to have attracted the odd and curious in others. One day, walking in the Piazza of Covent Garden, he was approached by a battered-looking fellow who pulled off his hat and requested permission to speak to him. Tennyson stopped. The man said: 'I've been drunk for three days and I want to make a solemn promise to you, Mr Tennyson, that I won't do it any more'. Tennyson muttered that this was a very praiseworthy resolve and that he hoped he would keep to it. The man said: 'I promise you I will, Mr Tennyson'. There was a moment's embarrassed silence and then the man added: 'Might I shake your hand?' Having done so, the man thanked the poet once more and went on his way.

It was fitting that he should have chosen the Laureate to be his confessor. Tennyson had a deep love and tolerance for all mankind. This was wonderfully illustrated the night the young A. M. Brookfield came to dine. His reputation for being rather a wayward child, perhaps even a little delinquent, had preceded him and Tennyson took him off to his study where he enquired after his favourite reading. Brookfield named the works of Mary Elizabeth Braddon, a prolific author of sensational thrillers. Tennyson confessed that he too was 'simply steeped in Miss Braddon – I am reading every word she ever wrote'.*

Brookfield went on to confide that the book of Miss Braddon's

*As he is known to have been an admirer of that other popular novelist, Marie Corelli, this may very well have been true.

which held the greatest appeal for him was the one in which, in the final chapter, all the people who were supposed to have been murdered suddenly reappeared, muttering: 'Not so, not so'. Tennyson thought this vastly clever.

At some point during the evening, the young man looked round for his host – perhaps in the hope of having some further conversation about Miss Braddon. Lady Tennyson was gently infoıming him that Lord Alfred had retired to his study to work and would not again come downstairs when the poet suddenly appeared, smoking his pipe and muttering: 'Not so, not so'.

Younger children sometimes found Tennyson's company more irritating. Whilst he claimed to hate being noticed, he invariably adopted a manner of dress – a large black sombrero and a voluminous cloak – calculated to attract attention. One of these cloaks, made for him in 1840, was still serving him thirty years later. It is now in the Usher collection at Lincoln. One day, walking hand in hand with the eight-year-old daughter of a friend, he was complaining at being pointed at when the little girl interrupted him. 'Perhaps, sir,' she said

'if you cut your hair and dressed like other people, they wouldn't stare so much.'

In *A Victorian Peep Show*, E. F. Benson tells two stories of Lord Tennyson at Marlborough House. The first concerns Oscar Browning, who approached him at a garden party and attempted to introduce himself by saying: 'Good afternoon, I'm Browning'. Tennyson said: 'No, you're not' and turned his back on him.

At a subsequent garden party, the poet found himself sharing a seat with a young and pretty admirer. She was so overcome by his presence that she could think of nothing to say. Lord Alfred had no small talk either. At last, and with what seemed like a superhuman effort, he said: 'Your stays creak'. Frightened by this rather personal remark, the lady hurried off. She had not gone far, however, before she observed that the poet was following her. In an attempt to evade him she fluttered from group to group, flitted from tree to tree. But his Lordship – like the Light Brigade – came ever onward. Flushed and flustered, her heart pounding in her throat, she turned at last into an avenue from which there was no escape. Tennyson was quickly at her side. 'I do beg your pardon' he said. 'It was my braces.'

If Lord Tennyson was eccentric in his dress he was surpassed by Dr Gunion Rutherford, for many years headmaster of Westminster School. Rutherford invariably wore a long, full-sleeved black robe and this occasionally caused misunderstandings. After one school function he was approached by a myopic peer who grasped his arm and steered him out of the room, murmuring: 'My dear, our carriage has come'. He seems to have lived in an academic world entirely divorced from reality and once startled a class by saying: 'I thought people were *born* knowing the date of the battle of Leuctra'.

With the exception in modern times of the admirable Colonel Wintle, eccentricity has been conspicuous in the army by its absence. One soldier who was ruined by it, however, was that 'hare-brained, half-cracked sort of fellow', Colonel Disney sometime *aide-de-camp* to the Duke of Cumberland. One day, Colonel Disney accompanied his master to Windsor, where the duke had gone to pay his respects to his royal parents. According to Gronow, the weak-bladdered Colonel:

finding waiting rather irksome, commenced making a tour through the apartments and in his peregrinations entered Her Majesty's bedchamber, which was rightly held to be sacred ground. Curiosity led him to inspect the various toilet articles of the Queen, and still further to examine a gold vase, which he put to a use which cannot be named to ears polite. This breach of good manners was detected by the royal housekeeper, the Hon. Miss Townshend, who, with tears in her eyes, reported to the Duke of Cumberland the gross impropriety. His Royal Highness, a proud overbearing man, sought out Disney and attempted to inflict summary chastisement for the insult he had perpetrated; however, the Colonel evaded the punishment so richly deserved, but he was almost immediately placed on the shelf.

Colonel Disney died in his lodgings 'heartbroken, on the second anniversary of his thoughtless freak'. As the royal family was then considered almost sacred, his death was interpreted as divine retribution. If he had heeded Fanny Burney's rather eccentric advice on how to conduct oneself before royalty, things might have ended differently:

> In the first place you must not cough. If you find a cough tickling in your throat, you must arrest it from making any sound; if you find yourself choking from the forebearance, you must choke – but not cough.
>
> In the second place you must not sneeze. If you have a vehement cold, you must take no notice of it; if your nose membranes feel a great irritation, you must hold your breath; if a sneeze still insists on making its way, you must oppose it, by keeping your teeth grinding together; if the violence of the repulse breaks some blood-vessels, then you must break the blood-vessel – but not sneeze.
>
> In the third place, you must not, upon any account, stir either hand or foot. If, by any chance, a black pin runs into your head, you must not take it out. If the pain is very great, you must be sure to bear it without wincing; if it brings the tears into your eyes, you must not wipe them off; if they give you a tingling by running down your cheeks, you must look as if nothing was the matter. If

> the blood should gush from your head by means of the black pin, you must let it gush; if you are uneasy to think of making such a blurred appearance, you must be uneasy, but you must say nothing about it. If, however, the agony is very great, you may, privately, bite the inside of your cheek, or of your lips, for a little relief; taking care, meanwhile, to do it so cautiously as to make no apparent dent outwardly. And with that precaution, if you even gnaw a piece out, it will not be minded, only be sure either to swallow it, or commit it to a corner of the inside of your mouth till they are gone – for you must not spit.

Other parts of the world ordered things differently and foreign potentates who became too attached to English traditions often found themselves in deep trouble. One such was King Amanullah of Afghanistan. Just after the Great War he stayed for a time at the Ritz Hotel in Piccadilly where he became the object of much interest. Lord Londonderry thought his entourage: 'the biggest gang of cut-throats I have seen in my life' and suspected that the King had been obliged to bring them along because if he had 'left them behind they would have usurped his throne'. None of the party spoke much English and when one of their number dismissed the pictures at Buckingham Palace as 'Worthless, quite worthless', there was an awkward silence until an interpreter explained that what he meant, of course, was 'priceless'. On his return home, King Amanullah attempted to pass a law requiring all his male subjects to wear bowler hats. They didn't take kindly to the idea and forced him to give way to someone less impressionable.

Chapter 4

Three Giants, Three Dwarfs and One Brute

A great deal has been written about the Mitford family in the past decade. As a result, there is now a tendency in certain quarters to denigrate the myth. A counter culture has grown up to which, when they are manifestly bored by it all, even the girls themselves subscribe. Recently, the youngest of the clan, Debo (now the rather imposing Duchess of Devonshire), told a reporter: 'The whole thing was an invention of my sister, Jessica. There was a family like ours in every village'. This, of course, is not true.

The co-founder of the Mitford dynasty was David Bertram Ogilvy Mitford, second Baron Redesdale, but known to his children as Farve. Bucolic and intolerant, he was blessed with a strong xenophobic streak and especially detested 'the filthy Hun' whom he never forgave for killing his brother Clem in the war. He was contemptuously dismissive of anyone whose skin was not quite white and when one of his female relatives married an Argentinian of impeccable – but Spanish – descent, Farve broke the news to his family by saying: 'I hear Robin's married a black'. In fact, Robin had forfeited Farve's good opinion years previously by arriving for a swimming party in a two-piece bathing costume. He remarked: 'I don't know why Robin finds it necessary to expose her very indifferent middle'.

Born in 1878, David Mitford served with great gallantry throughout the Boer War, suffering wounds which cost him the use of a lung. On his return to civilian life he took over the job of managing *The Lady*. It is difficult to think of anyone less suited to the task. He had no interest in feminine pursuits and no facility for journalism. He never read a book and when one of his daughters discovered the father of one of her friends deeply engrossed in some thick tome, she expressed surprise: 'I've never heard of a *man* reading a book'. Farve spent most of his time roaming the building with his pet mongoose, hunting rats. Years later, he was to hunt his children in much the same manner, giving them a ten-minute start before setting off in pursuit, accompanied by his faithful bloodhound.

The owner of '*The Lady*' at this time was Thomas Gibson Bowles, known to everyone as 'Cap'en Tommy'. In 1887 Cap'en Tommy was widowed and left with four young children to bring up. Believing that Jews tended to have a greater tolerance to disease, he did so according to Mosaic law. His two daughters, Sydney and Dorothy, were both required to wear sailor suits until they were seventeen when they were sent out to purchase 'one grown-up gown' which had to conform in style to those worn at the Court of Versailles a hundred and fifty years earlier.

Cap'en Tommy never took a bath – which he dismissed as 'nothing more than sitting in dirty water' – preferring to repair to his London club for a steam bath. If for any reason he was forced to leave London, he carried with him a set of dog kennels. When he wanted to perform his ablutions these were spaced out to form a line about fifty yards long. The smallest, lined with bricks, acted as the steam chamber. After about fifteen minutes, Cap'en Tommy would emerge from this and run like a demented lobster for 'the finishing line' while his footmen emptied buckets of ice-cold water over his head from positions atop the remaining kennels.

When Cap'en Tommy's daughter Sydney married David Mitford, her sister Dorothy remained behind in Lowndes Square to look after her eccentric father. One morning, he suddenly announced that he intended to emigrate to China – 'on Thursday'. Dorothy was commanded to close up the house, put the furniture into store, dismiss the servants and pack. She encompassed all this in three days and was dutifully sitting in the four-wheeler which was to convey them to the railway station, when her father descended the steps, held out his hand, palm upwards, and announced: 'My dear child, it's raining. We won't go'.

David Mitford's marriage to Sydney Bowles produced seven children: six girls and a boy named Tom, christened 'Tuddemey' by his sisters from a mistaken belief that it rhymed with 'adultery'. The girls fell naturally into two groups. The junior one was made up of Unity, Jessica and Debo. By the time they were born, their sisters Nancy, Pam and Diana were well on the way to being grown up.

In 1916 and at the age of thirty-eight, Farve succeeded as the second Baron Redesdale. Ten years later, he constructed a large mansion about a mile and a half from the Cotswold village of Swinbrook.

Life at Swinbrook House was completely self-contained. The house had its own schoolroom, riding-stables, tennis courts and laundry. Except for occasional trips into Burford or Oxford, the younger children saw almost nothing of the outside world. This tacit form of imprisonment was very irksome; but it unquestionably helped to mould their extraordinary characters.

Unity, Jessica and Debo were educated at home by a series of governesses whose salaries were paid from the profits of Lady Redesdale's chicken farm, managed by the aptly named Mr Lay. They were unruly and high-spirited children and few of these governesses stayed long. The second had to be dismissed after using one of her little charges as a battering-ram; and another, Miss Whiteley, had an aversion to snakes. Unity, who had a terrifying facility for laying bare adult weakness, entwined Enid, her pet grass snake, around the link-chain of the toilet. Miss Whiteley emitted a terrified shriek and fell off the seat in a dead faint. A workman had to be called to prise the door off its hinges in order to release her.

Miss Whiteley was succeeded by the angelic-looking Miss Buntin who taught the girls the theory and practice of shop-lifting. Her methods were crude but effective. She would descend with her pupils on the Oxford shops where one of them would stuff bags, pockets and underclothes with contraband while the remainder created the maximum distraction and confusion.

Although Miss Bunting was nominally in charge of the schoolroom, there were certain subjects in which Muv chose to instruct her children personally. She had inherited at least some of her odd beliefs from her father and her view of history was biased. She pointed out that while the territories of the British Empire were always coloured a 'lovely pink' on the map, those belonging to Germany were 'a hideous muddy, brown colour'. She also believed that children only draw from their lessons what they need to retain. One day, she requested Jessica – known as 'Decca' or 'Little D' – to read a passage from a book. When she had done so, she was asked to repeat what she had learned in her own words. This was not very much. Adopting her best coaxing manner, Muv said: 'Come now, Little D., can't you remember a single word?' After a moment of torn silence, Jessica said: 'Very well then – The'.

Muv had a feudal, almost medieval, attitude to life. She refused to have tinned food in the house and was implacably opposed to vaccination. 'What is the point of pumping dead germs into the system?' she said. 'Leave the Good Body to its own devices. It always provides a remedy in the end.' When Jessica broke her arm, the doctor set the bone and encased it in a sling. As soon as he had gone, Muv made Jessica remove this and perform a series of strenuous exercises with the injured limb so that 'it shouldn't get stiff'.

Farve shared Lady Redesdale's dislike of doctors. When the infant Nancy developed a foot infection which required lancing, he grudgingly agreed to call a doctor but insisted on overseeing the operation. Nancy was allergic to the anaesthetic and at one point her breathing grew very shallow and almost stopped. Years later, when someone asked Farve how he had reacted to this, he said: 'I seized the doctor by the neck and shook him like a rat'.

He would have felt no compunction in behaving like this because, as lord of the manor, he considered the doctor no more than a jumped-up family servant. He regarded the parson in much the same light. He held the right to dispose of the 'living' at Swinbrook and when it fell vacant interviewed candidates in person. In typically forthright fashion he informed them that he wanted no High Church rot at Swinbrook. He would continue to choose all the hymns himself. These would be solidly English – 'Jerusalem', 'Rock of Ages', that sort of thing. Each Thursday he would send over the subject for the following week's sermon. This should never over-run. If it looked like doing so, he would indicate a three-minute period of grace by raising the appropriate number of fingers. If this was disregarded: 'I shall precipitate you out of the pulpit by the scruff of your neck'.

Candidates for the living were interviewed by 'the Old Sub-Human' in his study, nicknamed by Jessica the Closing Room because the balance of probabilities suggested that as he spent so much of his life closeted within its four walls he would close his eyes there for the last time.

Lord Redesdale hated all young men. He particularly hated the friends of his daughters, whom he referred to as 'Damned Sewers.' One of these so annoyed him that the three younger girls cornered the lad in the library and sang him a chorus of 'We don't want to lose you but we think you ought to go'.

He only once waived this dislike: in the case of a young man called Mark. One of Nancy's particular friends, Mark was an 'arty' – a foppish aesthete of timid disposition and uncertain constitution. He was seldom at his best before mid-day when he would force down a cup of weak china tea.

Farve was very much a 'hearty'. One morning, as he had done each day for twenty years, he entered the breakfast room at exactly eight o'clock, crossed to the sideboard and lifted the lids of the various dishes. Having inspected them he crossed to his chair, pausing to slap Mark on the back. 'Brains for breakfast, Mark', he shouted. 'Brains for breakfast.' Mark turned bright green and left the room. The incident greatly amused Unity, Jessica and Debo who rushed about the house for days afterwards, shouting: 'Brains for breakfast, Mark: Brains for breakfast! Oh, the Damned Sewer! Oh, the Damned Sewer!'

As the eldest child, Nancy became something of a trail-blazer for the others and had often to bear the brunt of her father's displeasure. When she had her hair shingled there was a terrible row and no one talked to anyone else for a week. When she acquired a ukelele, an instrument which Farve thought 'fast', he threatened to disinherit her. Smoking was even more 'fast'. A copy of Stanley Spencer's *Resurrection* – a painting which depicts strange-looking semi-clad people issuing from their coffins on the Day of Judgement – caused the worst row of the lot.

By the time the younger children had begun to grow up these domestic upheavals were commonplace. Baiting 'the Old Sub-Human' provided a never-ending source of amusement. Unity devised a table-game which never failed to annoy him. She would shovel great quantities of food into her mouth without once removing her eyes from his face. Farve always attempted to stare her out. But never succeeded. When he could bear it no longer, he would crash his fists down on the table, causing the cutlery to tinkle and dance, and roar: 'Stop *looking* at me, damn you!'

Unity had always been good at devising things. In the nursery she invented an invisible *alter-ego* named 'Madame'. If she was accused of a misdemeanour, she would cry: 'But Nanny, "Madame" did it. I *saw* her'. Her favoured reading was *Sporting Life* and her spare time was spent picking fleas from the coat of her pet dachshund, Jacob. She was innately rebellious and had been forced to leave one school after appending the word 'rot' to a prize-day recitation of the line 'A garden is a lovesome thing, God wot'.

Debo had some equally absorbing past-times. When she was not checking through the still-births in *The Times*, she could be found squatting in the chicken-run in an effort to imitate the exact expression of pained concentration adopted by the egg-laying chickens. She was an extraordinarily sentimental girl and her sisters invented heart-rending stories with which to reduce her to tears. These were soon forbidden. But as all three knew the stories by heart, Unity and Jessica had only to whisper the opening line to achieve the same result as a full recitation.

This strong sibling rivalry had its roots in their disparate personalities: each one was quite unique. They were also physically odd. Nancy, Diana and Unity were all exceptionally tall. Debo, Jessica and Pamela were short. When a census enumerator asked Debo to describe the occupants of Swinbrook House, she replied: 'Three Giants, Three Dwarfs and One Brute'.

The 'Brute' was not Farve but Tom who, as the only boy, was rather ostracised by the others. Years after they had all grown up, Muv found an old cardboard badge inscribed around the circumference in a childish hand: 'League against Tom. Head: Nancy'.

Tom was often the good-natured butt of his sisters' games, some of which were fiendishly unpleasant. One of these was Slowly Working Away, which required the practitioner to engage her potential victim in a conversation of such riveting quality that he failed to notice that his companion was surreptitiously scratching at one spot on the back of his hand until blood was drawn.

A game which evolved from Slowly Working Away entailed pinching the fleshy part of the opponent's upper arm between thumb and forefinger whilst reciting 'Hure Hare Hure Commencement'. If the victim could withstand the ever-increasing pressure until this magical incantation had been repeated four times, he was adjudged the winner. Jessica was so impressed with 'Hure Hare Hure Commencement' that she asked Tom, who was studying law, to look into the possibility of copyrighting it.

Swinbrook's equivalent to William Brown, Jessica was the inspiration for most of these games. She also devised an exercise calculated to prepare her father for the onset of old age. When he was drinking his morning tea she would take his wrist between thumb and forefinger and gently shake it. She termed this 'Palsy Practice'. 'In a few years, when you're really old' she said 'you'll probably have palsy. I must give you a little practice now, before you actually get it, so that you won't be dropping things all the time.'

Life at Swinbrook House was occasionally enlivened by visits from relatives. One of the most welcome was Uncle Jack, a homosexual, whose marriage was never consummated and eventually annulled on the grounds of what the court chose to describe as 'masculine indolence'. One of the funniest was Uncle Tommy. Tommy was Farve's brother and every bit as forthright. He was also a local magistrate. When someone told him that he might in the course of his duties be required to attend a hanging, but could if he wished nominate a professional witness to go in his place, Tommy retorted: 'Pay someone to go to the theatre? I should say not'.

With the blood of Cap'en Tommy coursing through their veins, Muv's relations were equally odd. Her brother believed that England's greatness waxed and waned in direct ratio to the quantity of manure in the soil; and a sad and unfulfilled maiden aunt was said as a young girl to have contracted a disease of the gums which caused all her teeth to fall out. The younger children were fascinated by this and begged their mother to reveal all. Muv said: 'For many months she managed to hold them in with bits of bread, but it didn't work . . . now run along, that's all I'm going to tell you'.

If, as Jessica has suggested, she and her sisters were like a group of 'ill-assorted animals tied to a common tethering post', that post was now beginning to work loose. The first to achieve independence was Nancy. She had grown into a pretty young woman, tall, perfectly groomed, with a slender boyish figure and thick curly dark hair. Jessica thought she resembled 'an elegant pirate's moll'. She cultivated an Edwardian drawl – pronouncing 'off' as 'orf' and 'family planning' as 'fairmily plyennin' – which remained with her all her life. Her relationship with Farve continued to resemble a knockabout music-hall turn and he never quite forgave her extravagance or taste for the exotic. When Muv ran a competition to see who could produce the best-balanced budget for a pair of newly-weds surviving on £500 a year, Nancy put at the top of her list: 'Flowers . . . £490.'

She had always cherished the idea of being a writer and to this end cultivated a friendship with Evelyn Waugh, who thought her 'a nice cheap girl to take to a nightclub because she only drinks orangeade'. Her first novel *The Pursuit of Love* which she based on life at Swinbrook and in which Farve appeared thinly disguised as 'Uncle Matthew' and Muv as 'Aunt Sadie', was hugely popular. It ultimately sold more than a million copies. Its success left Nancy free to indulge her ingenuous and rather unworldly enthusiasm for high living. After the war she settled just outside Paris and became the epitome of the French Lady Novelist – poised, confident and never photographed except on some fragile gold chair with an ormolu clock in the background.

Before she was eighteen, Nancy's younger sister, the beautiful Diana, had fallen in love with Bryan Guinness. Farve opposed the marriage on the grounds that Bryan's parents were in trade. He said: 'I suppose they will want to put her on a poster advertising their blasted beer'. Diana, who was tall and athletic and rather resembled 'a Vogue cover-artist's conception of the Goddess of the Chase', got her way by sulking for the entire winter. Jessica wondered whether she was really sulking or just 'practising being frightfully rich'.

Despite the difference in their ages, Jessica and Diana had always been close. At one point the older girl had attempted to teach her little sister to ride. Jessica had a tendency to keep falling off. This mildly annoyed Diana who said: 'Do try to hang on this time, darling. You know how cross Muv will be if you break your arm again'. Muv took comfort from the Good Body's ability to look after itself. She said: 'Oh, dear. Poor Little D. She doesn't seem to have much bounce'.

Pamela, the least written about of all the girls, made up this triumvirate of older sisters. 'Her birth' said Nancy 'threw me into a rage which lasted twenty years.' Pam spent her childhood joyously and stolidly immersed in the ways of the country, regularly accompanying her father on shoots. As a result, she acquired the nickname 'Palmer' from one of the gamekeepers who found it impossible to pronounce 'Pamela'. She was also known as 'Wombling', 'Woo' or 'Woman'.

Just as Debo spent long hours imitating chickens, so Pam longed to be a horse. She could usually be found in the paddock or stables, whinnying, tossing her head and pawing the ground. When she discovered she couldn't be a horse, she did the next best thing – married a jockey and employed a solicitor named Withers. She is today something of a gourmet and her sisters believe she can recall every meal she has ever eaten. The only Mitford to retain her Cotswold roots, she strongly resembles Edith Evans in the role of Miss Marple.

Unlike Pamela, Jessica hated life at Swinbrook and resolved to escape at the first opportunity. At the age of ten she wrote to the family bankers, Messrs Drummond, and received the following reply:

> 'We respectfully beg leave to acknowledge
> receipt of ten shillings as initial deposit
> in your Running Away Account.'

Jessica took great delight in showing this letter to her parents, who should have been forewarned. A decade later, she made the acquaintance of her second cousin, Esmond Romilly, whom she immediately recognised as a kindred spirit. A nephew of Sir Winston Churchill, from whom he seems to have inherited much of his spirit and pugnacity, Romilly had been educated at Wellington School where he reduced the staff to a state of apoplexy by inserting pacifist literature into the hymn books shortly before a service of remembrance. At the age of fifteen he absconded from Wellington, establishing an underground information centre in Bloomsbury for like-minded runaways. Having persuaded George Bernard Shaw to put up the money, he also founded a left-wing magazine aimed at other intelligent but rebellious schoolboys. The quality of this was so good that the authorities at Wellington banned it. Nonetheless it continued to circulate clandestinely and sold throughout the country more than three thousand copies in the course of a year.

One night Romilly turned up drunk at the home of his parents.

Arrested for disorderly behaviour, he was found to be beyond parental control and sent to a home for delinquents. After six weeks he was released into the care of a distant relative. In 1936, when civil war broke out in Spain, he decamped to join the International Brigade.

A few months later he was invalided home. He returned to the house of the lady who had taken him in after his release from the home for delinquent boys and here he met Jessica. His reputation had preceded him and Jessica fell instantly and violently in love. When Esmond announced that he was thinking of returning to Spain – had been offered an advance of ten pounds to act as war correspondent for a daily newspaper – Jessica begged him to take her with him.

They drew out the fifty pounds in the Running Away Account and fled to join the anti-Franco forces. When news of her elopement reached Swinbrook – which because of the sly way they had arranged matters was not for some weeks – Farve had his daughter made a Ward of Court. Nancy wrote: 'Everyone sent flowers. It was just like a funeral. You are the first one to be on posters. Unity was frightfully jealous'.

Nancy and her husband, Peter Rodd, went to France to persuade the runaways to return. As it was known that they were destitute and very close to starvation, Eden sent a warship to lure Jessica on board with the promise of a sumptuous meal. She became suspicious and refused. The couple were eventually married by the British Consul at Bayonne. Farve never forgave Jessica her 'disloyalty' and when he died, left her nothing. Each of his bequests was qualified with the words 'except Jessica'.

The name of the 'frightfully jealous' Unity was also now beginning to figure prominently in the headlines. She had become a fanatical pro-Nazi and astonished the people of Swinbrook by goose-stepping around the village, greeting the vicar and the postmistress with the raised-arm Nazi salute. In January 1935 she flew to Germany to make the acquaintance of Hitler. She sat for days in the *Cafe Osteria Bavaria* staring at him with the same fierce intensity formerly reserved for Farve. Her statuesque appearance, her flaxen hair and the fact that she spoke fluent German – albeit with a slight Bavarian accent – rendered her an object of interest. Hitler invited her to his table. She had a good singing voice and was soon confiding to him that she longed to sing Elsa in *Lohengrin*.

It is difficult to understand the mental and moral processes which allowed her to sublimate the implications of Nazism. It may be that her insular upbringing provided her with no natural defences against extreme political creeds. Despite her notorious anti-semitism, she was not at heart a political creature. Her real infatuation was less with the Nazi doctrine than with Hitler himself.

Hitler's motives for cultivating Unity are uncertain. One can only assume that he had an exaggerated idea of the role minor aristocrats played in the running of the country. He was flattered by Unity's admiration and allowed her to accompany him to the Munich Olympic Games. He also permitted her to introduce her family. Despite a lifelong detestation of 'the filthy Hun', Farve became an enthusiastic convert. Jessica, alone, was not surprised. 'Farve' she said 'is really one of Nature's fascists.'

Diana also fell under the Nazi spell. She and Bryan Guinness had outlived their youthful infatuation; and in 1936, following a quiet divorce, Diana married Sir Oswald Mosley, the leader of the British Union of Fascists. As a result of their political views, both husband and wife were imprisoned during the Second World War, Diana for three and a half years. For some time afterwards Sir Oswald was refused a passport.

When it became clear that the alliance between Germany and England for which she longed was impossible, Unity's fragile world collapsed. Tom was asked what he thought she would do. Understanding the extent of her romantic idealism, he said: 'I think she will shoot herself'. He was right. In a mood of black despair she repaired to Munich's *Englische Garten* where she put a bullet in her head. It did not kill her – at least, not directly or at once – and she was invalided home to Swinbrook where she finally expired. Her funeral was a sad and lonely business. A creature of the Lost Weekend, she had lived a life entirely circumscribed by two world wars: born just four days after England came to blows with the Kaiser, she died, at least in spirit, in September 1939.

With the coming of the Second World War the old order began to fade. Esmond Romilly was killed in action and Jessica, the only left-wing member of the family, made a new life for herself in America. She became a writer, the scourge of American undertakers, and married a radical lawyer. In 1955, after a sixteen-year separation, she was reunited with Nancy, who presented her with a cheque for £50, saying: 'I took over your furniture when you left'. As Jessica conceded, the 'furniture' consisted of 'five or six Left Book Club volumes and a couple of cushions', but it was typical that Nancy should have found a way of sharing her success without appearing to bestow charity. She had displayed a similar tenderness towards Unity after the suicide attempt; but she detested what she called 'the hideous taste' of the new world and could hardly wait to be out of it. In the summer of 1973, after four years of suffering 'wrong diagnosis and wrong treatment', she died of Hodgkin's disease, a form of lymph cancer. Sharp-tongued and sarcastic, profoundly reserved yet fundamentally kind and supportive, she had been a contagiously cheerful friend to her sisters and was sadly missed.

After their release from prison, Diana and Sir Oswald Mosley purchased a *directoire* country estate called the Temple of Glory at Orsay, just outside Paris, where they lived for the remaining thirty years of Sir Oswald's life. Lady Mosley has never succumbed to paranoia or a sense of martyrdom and traces of her great beauty still remain. Her sister Debo recently remarked that she is 'the only one of us with a real face'. Like her sister Jessica, she has turned herself into a proficient writer, regularly contributing reviews to *Books and Bookmen*. Like Nancy, she pronounces certain words with a decidedly old-fashioned inflection, saying 'crawss' for 'cross' and 'gels' for 'girls'. Rather inappropriately for such an authoritarian old lady, she is known to her sisters as 'Honks'.

While still relatively young, Debo married Andrew Cavendish who in 1950 succeeded to the Dukedom of Devonshire on the death of his elder brother. The youngest of the six girls, she had always nurtured the ambition to marry a duke. When one of her sisters was bemoaning the lack of eligible suitors, Muv consoled her by saying: 'Never mind, dear. I'm sure Mr Right will come along'. Debo said: 'Or the Duke of Right'.

As Duchess of Devonshire, Debo has ruled over Chatsworth House – her husband's country-seat in Derbyshire, and the model for 'Pemberley' in *Pride and Prejudice* – for thirty years. The days when even the exterior windows were gilded with gold leaf are long gone. The present owners refer to the house as 'the Dump' and compare its administration to 'a cross between running Claridge's and the British Museum'. In moments of severe depression, Debo recalls the advice of Harold Macmillan, who said that if she were foolish enough to take it on she would never again be able to turn away a boring relative on the grounds that she lacked a spare bed.

She admits, however, that there are 'certain compensations'. She finds business 'absolutely gripping' and runs two shops which help support the estate: one selling meat and vegetables, the other Chatsworth souvenirs. She is a woman of strong views and once said: 'If I were Dictator, everything in the countryside would be painted black'. She has a preference for wooden lavatory seats – 'Nicer than Habitat, don't you think, and cheaper' – and as the house has more than fifty water closets the estate carpenters are kept fully employed.

There are regular house-parties at Chatsworth and Princess Margaret's name frequently figures on the guest list. Two days prior to one of her visits, Sir Alec Douglas-Home slept in the room she was due to occupy. He told his hostess: 'If I lie very still and don't turn over, you won't have to change the sheets'.

Like her father, Debo has no interest in books. Her reading is confined to bloodstock pedigrees and lists. Knowing this, Evelyn Waugh once sent her a copy of one of his novels with the title engraved on the spine, but the leaves blank. She has also inherited her father's insularity and has little time for what she calls 'Abroad'. She seldom goes to London and most of her clothes are bought off the peg at agricultural shows. Her husand is quietly amused by the legend which has grown up around his wife and her sisters and refers to the musical based on·their lives as 'La Triviata'.

Once their children had left home, Lord and Lady Redesdale came to realise that they had very little in common. Farve deserted Swinbrook House for a remote cottage at Otterburn in Northumberland where, in 1958, four days after his eightieth birthday, he died. He left an estate of £129,000 reduced after death duties to a mere £53,000. In its obituary *The Times* described him a man 'who adhered to somewhat old-fashioned views with tenacity and boisterousness'. It added that in contrast to the ladies of his family 'he was a rather shadowy personality' – proof, if ever it was needed, of Professor Haldane's view that you can believe nothing in a newspaper except the date.

Lady Redesdale did not long survive her husband and was buried beside him in Swinbrook churchyard. Their moss-encrusted headstone stands guard near the gate. West of the church, two grass humps mark the last resting-place of Unity the Nazi and Nancy the Novelist. Viewing them one is rather basely reminded of Nancy's visit to Russia in 1954, when she viewed the embalmed bodies of Lenin and 'Bonny Prince Stalin', which she thought looked 'like a dreadful old married couple'.

Inside the church are two further memorials: the Redesdale coat of arms; and the pews, donated by Farve from the proceeds of a long-since-forgotten win on the Grand National. Two miles away, at the top of the hill, Swinbrook House looks down towards the village. Although no Mitford lives there now, there is a rumour that some of Unity's childhood drawings still grace the walls. A Range Rover in the drive helps dispel something of the old-rashioned bleakness. But the Mitford imprint cannot be erased. One catches the echo of three voices chanting down the tunnel of sixty years: 'Brains for breakfast, Mark! Brains for breakfast! Oh, the Damned Sewer! Oh, the Damned Sewer!'

And Muv plaintively muttering: 'I know when I see *Peer's Daughter* in a headline, it's bound to be one of mine'.

Chapter 5

Nuts in Comfort: The Man Who Wouldn't Let Go

The life of Howard Hughes, unparalleled for its oddity, can be divided into two phases: the early decades dedicated to headline-grabbing exploits and high living; and the years spent as a recluse. Both, in their way, are densely encrusted with legend.

The most enduring of these is of Hughes the businessman: the entrepreneurial loner with the Midas touch. Like so many of the myths which surround him, it has no basis in fact. In a career spanning half a century, every project he essayed crumbled to dust beneath his fingers. He destroyed Trans World Airlines (TWA); brought the film studios of RKO to the verge of bankruptcy; and ruined what in more sensible hands must surely have been a highly profitable aircraft division – failing in the process to honour two vital war-time government contracts. As a result of his indiscriminate purchase of property he reduced Las Vegas to a slum; manufactured a number of second-rate films; and squandered more than two billion dollars on a series of projects as ludicrous and bizarre in their own way as Horatio Bottomley's 'Nil Desperandum Mine Company'. Despite assets of a hundred and fifty million dollars, he ended his days an insane drug-ridden recluse whose personal possessions amounted to no more than one pair of draw-string shorts and an old trilby hat.

According to Clarence A. Waldron, Howard Hughes was descended from a hardy breed of Anglo-Welsh farmers who emigrated to Virginia in 1607. His paternal great-grandfather, Joshua W. Hughes, became a redoubtable Indian hunter and was rewarded for his efforts with a government grant of forty acres of land in Scotland County, Missouri. Joshua's eldest son Felix became a lawyer and a superintendent of schools.

Felix's own son, Howard Hughes Sr, was born in 1869. He refused a safe desk job in his father's law firm and became instead an oil-field greaser, discarding his fine clothes and working alongside some of 'the roughest, most hardened men of his time'. He led a transient existence, flitting from one oil strike to the next. In May 1904 he married the pretty daughter of a prominent Texas judge. The judge's father – Howard Hughes' great-grandfather – was General Richard Gano, an extraordinary character in his own right. He fought with the Confederacy throughout the Civil War, surviving seventy battles and having five horses shot under him. As well as being a qualified doctor, he was an enthusiastic lay preacher and in a long life converted sixteen thousand men to the Baptist faith.

After his marriage, Howard Hughes Sr settled with his wife close to the stagnant waters of the Houston bayous where, on Christmas Eve 1905, Howard Robard Hughes Jr was born. It was a difficult birth which for some reason was never registered. As no official record of it has ever been found, it may be that Howard Hughes never really existed – was merely a figment of his own florid imagination.

Mining for oil in the southern states of America at the turn of the century was a difficult, dangerous and frustrating business. The antiquated fish-tail drill then in common use was competent enough when it came to boring through mud and silt, but hopeless the moment it encountered solid rock. Utilising various current ideas, Howard Sr set to work to devise a suitable alternative. He came up with what became known as 'the Hughes rock-eater'. Patented in 1909, it formed the basis of the Hughes billions and, only moderately refined, continues to enjoy a world-wide popularity to this day.

Shy and somewhat withdrawn, Howard Hughes Jr inherited his father's interest in the workings of intricate machinery. He found it less taxing than people. Before he was ten he had built a small radio transmitter from the components of the family doorbell. He later described this as 'one of the greatest thrills of my life'. In March 1922 his mother died – at the early age of thirty-nine. His father removed his sixteen-year-old son from school in order to have his companionship. The decision was to have a lasting and catastrophic effect on Howard's life. According to his teachers, he was a boy who badly 'needed to learn more about how to carry himself among other fellows'. Now he would never learn.

In January 1925, Howard Hughes Sr died of a massive heart attack at the age of fifty-four. Howard had thus lost both parents in the space of three years and at the age of eighteen found himself both an orphan and a millionaire. Unfortunately, and in the eyes of the law, he was still a minor and therefore disqualified from regulating his own affairs. His uncle Rupert attempted to put himself forward as his guardian. This led to a bitter dispute which ultimately alienated young Howard from his paternal relatives entirely. He petitioned the Texas Department of Justice to remove his 'disability of minority'. Claiming to be impressed by his knowledge of the oil industry, Judge Walter Montieth (who happened to be one of Howard's golfing partners) concurred. With control of his father's tool company safely in his pocket, Howard next bought up the minority holdings of his paternal relatives. Having done so, he promptly forgot them and never spoke to any of them again. He further asserted his independence by marrying Ella Rice, a childhood sweetheart who, at twenty-one, was two years his senior.

Within nine months of his father's death, Hughes moved to Hollywood with the notion of financing and ultimately producing silent movies. He invested sixty thousand dollars in a pot-boiler entitled *Swell Hogan* which proved so bad 'that it was never released'. His second film fared rather better and made a star of William Boyd, who went on to achieve a different kind of fame as Hopalong Cassidy.

Late in 1927 Hughes started work on *Hell's Angels*, a film based on the valorous exploits of First World War aviators. The shooting of the aerial sequences proved a highly dangerous business and in striving to placate the producer's ever-increasing demands for 'realism', three pilots and a mechanic lost their lives. When he insisted on taking up a Morse scout plane for an unauthorised spin, Hughes himself suffered a nasty and near-fatal accident which left him requiring extensive facial surgery. This, together with his intense involvement with his work, placed an unbearable strain on his marriage. During the months of filming – firstly in the California desert and later on the indoor lot at Metropolitan studios – Ella Hughes was afforded a glimpse of an obsessive side to her husband's character which she found rather frightening. In October 1928 she left him. They never lived together again and were divorced shortly before Christmas 1929.

Hell's Angels established Hughes overnight. He became Hollywood's darling – a whizz-kid endowed with boundless talent, toughness, daring and determination. He also became the movie capital's most eligible bachelor. His name was linked romantically with several well-known actresses, including Billie Dove and Carole Lombard.

He followed *Hell's Angels* with another box-office success: *Scarface* – a thinly veiled account of Al Capone and the Chicago mob. He always remained particularly attached to this picture and after its initial distribution locked it away in a subterranean vault for forty years, refusing all offers – many of them very lucrative – for its re-release.

In 1932, and at the pinnacle of his fame, Hughes abruptly abandoned his movie career for an even grander obsession: aeronautics. He had acquired his pilot's licence in 1928 and now, in order to gain valuable experience, signed up with a commercial airline as a co-pilot, using an assumed name. It was the only time in his life he worked for anyone else. His identity was discovered after one flight.

Shortly afterwards he won his first aviation race; and he constructed the H-I, an aeroplane in which, on 13th September 1935, he set a new world-speed record of three hundred and fifty-two miles per hour. Three months later he wrested the transcontinental title from Roscoe Turner; and in January 1937 he shaved two and a half hours off his former time, establishing a record which would stand for the best part of a decade.

If it was a remarkable achievement, it was not enough. In July 1938 the 'aviator millionaire' set out to fly around the world. On the first leg of the journey – to Paris – he shattered Lindbergh's record by more than half and landed the following morning in Moscow. In the face of near impossible conditions, he battled on across Asia, arriving back in New York just three days, nineteen hours and seventeen minutes after leaving it. He was greeted by a cheering, near-hysterical crowd of thirty thousand people, every one of whom desired to shake his hand. Mayor La Guardia described the flight as 'the greatest achievement in the history of aviation'. A civic reception was arranged, which Howard ducked. The following day he was honoured with a tribute he could not duck: a ticker-tape parade along Broadway and Battery Hill, attended by more than a million frantic and elated New Yorkers. Howard Hughes was a national hero – and he hated it. It was the ultimate contradiction: the last private man driven by inner compulsions to indulge in exploits which could not help but bring publicity raining down upon his head.

In 1940 Hughes acquired a majority holding in TWA; and after an eight-year break returned to film-making with *The Outlaw*, a story loosely based on the life of Billy the Kid. The production transformed the mousey, raw-boned Jane Russell from an insignificant secretary and erstwhile Sunday-school teacher into one of the world's most enduring sex symbols. Hughes became obsessed with his leading lady's breasts and drew on his knowledge of aerodynamics to construct a special cantilevered bra for her which would display her impressive charms to full effect. She was photographed wearing this, beneath the flimsiest of blouses. Suitably blown up, the photograph was used to promote *The Outlaw* on a series of gigantic billboards across the country, Miss Russell reclining seductively in a haystack and fondling a Colt .45.

Shortly after the completion of *The Outlaw*, the Hughes Aircraft Company moved to Culver City, California, where work was begun on the D-2 – a plane which the Air Force swiftly rejected. As a result of his connections, the patriotic billionaire was next asked to build three flying-boats at a cost of eighteen million dollars. In May 1943, whilst undergoing trials, the S-43 crashed into Lake Mead, killing two of the crew. Hughes, who was piloting the machine, suffered extensive injuries. When he recovered, a further contract was issued for the building of a hundred reconnaissance planes – and subsequently cancelled. It was superceded by an order for another flying-boat which, when delivered, was dismissed by the Air Force as 'sub-standard'. All in all, the Hughes Aircraft Company had a bad war.

At its termination, Howard grew bored with money-making and like many a rich man before him, decided to focus his attention on acquiring the power which money represents. In the summer of 1949 he resolved to buy up Las Vegas and instructed his aides to lease a house from which the operation might be conducted in comfort. Once this had been achieved, he commissioned a team of engineers to design – at a cost of eighty thousand dollars – an air-humidifier which would counteract the dust which swept in at all times of the day and night from the Nevada desert.

As soon as the humidifier had been installed, Howard moved in accompanied by his valet, a man called Bruno, who repaired to the kitchen to prepare Hughes' lunch of steak and salad. When this was put in front of him, Hughes complained that the lettuce had wilted. Bruno replaced the offending leaves with some fresher ones. Unfortunately, the humidifier was so powerful that during the short journey from the kitchen to the table, these too wilted. Hughes stared morosely at his plate for some time. Then he said: 'Let's go'. Bruno knew better than to argue with his master's 'whim of steel'. As he later deposed: 'If Howard Hughes asked you to go and stand on your head in the corner, you didn't ask why. You asked: "Which corner?"' Within an hour they had departed.

Because none of his aides were allowed to refer to any matter which had not first been raised by the boss, the rent on the property, a sum in excess of a quarter of a million dollars, continued to be paid for seven years. When Hughes at last thought to terminate the lease, he sent two of his top executives to the house to clear up. They found his steak exactly where he had abandoned it, covered in a disgusting green fungus.

Shortly afterwards, the billionaire leased a house in Palm Springs. He left after a few days but issued instructions that the air-conditioning should be left running as he intended to return almost at once. He never did. But as no orders were issued to the contrary, the motor continued to whir for eight years. After two years the ceilings collapsed. Three years later the plaster fell off the walls. When the property was eventually handed back to its rightful owner it was in a state of virtual ruin. Hughes witheld compensation for decades.

This total lack of consideration for the possessions of others was exceeded in Hughes only by a holy passion for acquiring something for nothing. He borrowed expensive limousines from car dealers on free trial; and for some years employed a clerk to do nothing but write to charity-manufacturers with a view to obtaining hearing-aids on similar terms. He never paid for – and frequently never used – the items he gleaned in this way nor, unless the company threatened to sue, were they ever returned.

One time the 'billionaire miser' obtained a Super Constellation from the Lockheed Aircraft Corporation by hinting that he wished to purchase a similar aircraft for TWA. Being aware of his reputation, Lockheed thought to protect its interests by sending a representative along on the half-hour flight. Howard took the controls and flew the plane to Montreal where he announced that he had never had any intention of buying the machine, reinforcing this by entering into negotiations with a rival company for the purchase of British aircraft. He parked the Constellation broadside on to the runway and turned it into an office. The Lockheed man threatened to sue. When this had no effect, he announced that he would take the next flight home. With characteristic arrogance, Hughes refused to let him go. He said he needed him to advise on the negotiations with the British. When these were concluded – and instead of returning to base – Hughes flew on to the Bahamas, where he remained a full month. The aeroplane was returned to Lockheed fit only for scrap.

The first indication that Hughes' character might be starting to turn inwards was marked by a significant decrease in his phenomenal levels of energy. He issued instructions to the nucleus of his empire, at Romaine Street, that he should never be disturbed with messages if asleep 'or during the first two hours of being awake unless a real emergency'.

At that date the Romaine Street headquarters was staffed by men and women of integrity and efficiency. They were deeply loyal to their employer and did everything they could to further his interests. All this changed the night Hughes learned that one of his aircraft had been lost over central America. In an effort to glean information, he telephoned each of his senior aides by turn. As it was Christmas Eve, they were either out of town, otherwise unavailable or simply too drunk to come to the phone. The billionaire at last succeeded in contacting a relatively junior employee named Bill Gay. He asked Gay why he out of so many should be home and sober. Gay explained that he was a Mormon: forbidden by his religion to smoke, drink or indulge in high living. Hughes said nothing at the time but afterwards issued an instruction that all future employees were to be drawn from the ranks of the Mormons. 'The Mormon Mafia', as it came to be known, eventually took over the day-to-day running of his empire almost entirely.

Because he believed that all employees outside this cadre of senior aides were either simple-minded or corrupt, Hughes maintained a fleet of private detectives to check on them. These spying campaigns were orchestrated with discretion and efficiency by a man named Chouinard. Unfortunately, Hughes developed irrational aversions to certain detectives with the result that more than three hundred names were entered and subsequently deleted from the payroll in nineteen years. This exercise cost the billionaire two million dollars but, like most of his expenses, it seems to have been tax deductable. Hughes was a ferocious tax manipulator and on one occasion the Attorney General, Robert Kennedy, was forced to ask how it was that a man with a personal expenditure of two million dollars a year never paid more in taxes than five hundred dollars.

When Hughes' detectives were not engaged in spying on their fellow employees, they chaperoned various Hughes starlets – taking them shopping, or to photographic sessions, drama lessons and screen tests. Although he never seriously promoted the careers of any of these young hopefuls, our real-life Daddy Warbucks enjoyed having them around. He kept detailed case histories on a hundred and eight of them. They were maintained in a California-style purdah: closely guarded and never allowed out unaccompanied.

Nonetheless, breaches in security did occur. One day a starlet announced that she was abandoning her career to marry one of the Mormon chauffeurs. In order to prevent such a thing happening again, Hughes instructed his staff to dismiss all the heterosexual chauffeurs and recruit homosexual ones. This simply generated a fresh set of problems. Two of the new employees were arrested for kerb crawling and propositioning young men. Hughes sacked them: not for immorality, but for 'expressly disregarding my instructions about always driving in the middle of the road in order to avoid picking up leaf mould and other detritus on the tyres'. He had a special fear of this type of cross-contamination and whenever he stayed at hotels insisted that the trolley used to bring his meals to the room should remain outside the kitchen while the food was being prepared in case the wheels should accidentally pick up a cockroach.

A second starlet scandal involved a pretty fifteen-year-old blonde, with enormous breasts and big blue eyes, to whom Hughes had offered a part in some second-rate romance then being filmed on the lot at RKO. He was very protective towards her – she was to be his new Jane Russell – and issued precise instructions to the chauffeurs on how to proceed when driving her. In order to minimise damage to her breast tissue, they should avoid bumpy roads, slowing when crossing railway or tram lines to a speed of two miles an hour. The girl's mother, a calculating, grasping woman, quickly saw that Hughes had no intention of furthering anyone's interests but his own and having engineered him into a compromising situation with her daughter, burst into the bedroom and denounced him. Rather than risk exposure and scandal, the eccentric billionaire settled out of court for a figure rumoured to be in excess of a quarter of a million dollars.

When he tired of his protegees they were ruthlessly discarded. This caused a certain amount of resentment and he lived in fear of a subsequent chance encounter. To minimise the risk of this he took to sidling into restaurants and hotels via the back door and leaving by the fire escape, a habit which only served to increase his reputation for eccentricity and furtiveness.

Nonetheless he enjoyed playing the man-about-town. He bore a passing resemblance to Jimmy Stewart – as he appeared in *Mr Smith Goes to Washington* – and he was very popular with the ladies, who were attracted by his shyness. One year he announced that he wished to celebrate New Year by dining with three beautiful women in the Beverly Hills Hotel – but separately, with each girl believing she was his only companion. This took a certain amount of arranging. It was eventually agreed that the first girl should be entertained in the restaurant, the second in the Polo Lounge and the third in a private room. Having consumed a starter with the first girl, Hughes would be called away, ostensibly to receive a telephone call. He would then proceed to the table of the second girl, where the performance would be repeated. In this way each girl would suffer three interruptions to her meal and Howard would achieve his ambition.

Initially, all went according to plan. After the second interruption, however, the first girl – who happened to be Susan Hayward – became suspicious. On the pretext of going to powder her nose, she followed Hughes to the table of the second girl – who happened to be Jean Peters. The evening ended with all three girls berating Hughes in the hotel lobby. Susan Hayward vowed never to speak to him again – a promise she kept.

The anecdote not only demonstrates Hughes's love of manipulating people, but the bizarre lengths to which he was already prepared to go to attain his ends. He was intensely patriotic and another of his wayward schemes involved the dropping of propaganda leaflets over Russia. For some months he occupied himself with the logistics of this to the exclusion of all other business. It became his personal crusade against the evils of communism. He decided that the messages were to be inserted into cartons of cigarettes – tax deductable cigarettes – concealed in balloons. The balloons were to be transported to the Russian coast in the false bottoms of boats manned by Portuguese fishermen. They would then be inflated and released. Once they reached their destination they would be deflated by remote control. After several weeks of excited discussion and speculation, Hughes suddenly changed tack and never mentioned the project again.

Not all his obsessions died young. In certain situations he was capable of a terrifying single-mindedness.

For a time Hughes dated the actress Ava Gardner. When she became involved with Sinatra, she confessed to Hughes that he was maltreating her. Nothing could be done at the time; but some years later, when Hughes was acquiring land and property in Las Vegas and had become the State of Nevada's largest private employer, Sinatra offered to sell him certain holdings of his own. Hughes was enthusiastic; but every time Sinatra endeavoured to pin him to a contract, the billionaire was either unavailable to discuss the matter or raised irritating and trifling objections. After allowing the situation to develop over several weeks, he finally announced that he wanted nothing to do with the man or any of his projects.

The sale had meant a great deal to Sinatra who now went on the rampage, breaking up furniture in one of Hughes' hotels. A fight developed with another customer, and this Sinatra lost. He also lost several teeth and suffered extensive facial bruising. In a rare flash of humour, Hughes dubbed him: 'Old Black and Blue Eyes'.

If Hughes was implacable towards those he disliked, his benevolence often had even more unfortunate consequences. Perhaps because she was so often left to her own devices, Jean Peters formed an attachment to a rather mangy-looking tom-cat. One day it went missing. Hughes mounted a vast operation to look for it. He directed proceedings from his home, insisting on a progress report every hour. When the hunt failed to produce results, he flew into a rage, threatened to sack every last employee and bring in a specialist trapper from Africa. He sent his staff a thousand-word memo on the subject. Word-bound and intensely preoccupied with trivia, it was couched in rambling, ungrammatical phrases hardly recognisable as those of a man who, twenty years previously, had lectured his lawyers on 'not using the infinitive to express a major thought except as an auxiliary to the main verb':

> This is not the jungle; this is not the Everglades; this is not the New York City with the dense population. It is thinly populated and it is no problem at all to question all the people here and have them questioned by somebody and get at the truth and not permit somebody to conceal the truth just because they are afraid of being sued or something like that. Proper questions by people skilled in questioning could have been had. The animal could have been searched for by a team of people skilled in the ways of animals of this type. I know one thing: if the zoo had lost some valuable animal in this area, there would have been twenty-five or thirty men scouring the countryside, men skilled in the habits and ways of an animal of this kind and would have found it by now.

The creature was finally run to earth in a derelict barn. Hughes examined it and finding it an unsuitable addition to his household, interviewed several couples prepared to take it in. None were found acceptable. It went, instead, to a luxurious 'cattery' where it was installed in an individually decorated room, complete with television. As one of the rules of this establishment required that former owners write to their pets once a month, Howard hired an Australian named Harry to relieve him of the chore. Harry was still on the payroll at Howard's death.

The cat incident neatly illustrates the most bizarre of all Hughes' characteristics: his refusal to let go. He posted guards outside houses he never intended to lease. He leased hangars he never visited, stocked with aircraft he never flew. He kept aspiring young actresses 'on the hook'; and he eventually carried this philosophy of fierce proprietorship to its logical conclusion by developing a similar dog-in-the-manger attitude towards his own body. He refused to cut his finger-nails and acquired the odd nervous habit of clicking his long toenails together when dictating. When they broke off, he had them wrapped in cotton wool and placed in pill boxes. His urine was sealed in glass jars, each of which was carefully numbered, dated and catalogued. They were then stored in a nearby garage. Every so often an employee would be told: 'Go count the jars'. Howard knew exactly how many jars there should be and it was a bad day for anyone who failed to come up with the correct tally.

Despite his tendency to hire and fire, Howard's obsession with retention occasionally extended to his staff. For a time one of his aides was required to sit on the toilet adjacent to his room until summoned to take care of some trivial need. The task had to be performed in total silence and, because Hughes was developing scopophobia – a fear of being looked at – with eyes averted.

One day the man had just returned home after a ten-hour spell on duty when he received a telephone call urgently summoning him back. He drove like the wind and arrived in record time. Howard handed him a tape-measure and asked him to calculate by what degree the cushion on which he was leaning had slipped during his absence. Having done so, he was instructed 'to go home and get some rest'.

The man was ultimately made redundant by Howard's own need for the bathroom. The billionaire suffered from hideous constipation and once spent twenty-eight hours on the toilet. Towards the end of his life he became incapable of bearing the pain of a bowel movement without first having one of his doctors administer a rectal anaesthetic. This irregularity induced an appalling case of haemorrhoids which Jean Peters nagged him to have treated. After some resistance, he agreed to fly to a hospital in New England, but imposed one condition: Jean should attempt neither to visit him nor telephone the hospital during his stay.

On the appointed day, Howard left the house to board the airliner which would take him to New England. Instead, he drove to a small private screening room on Sunset Boulevard which belonged to the producer Martin Nosseck. Hughes had formerly done what he called his 'movie-screening' at the Goldwyn Studios; but when he learned that the theatre had once been used by the cast of *Porgy and Bess*, he never went back. He had a deep-rooted dislike and fear of negroes dating from the day in 1917 when a black contingent of the National Guard had run amuck in Houston, indiscriminately shooting whites. Seventeen people died before their advance could be halted and thirteen of the soldiers were later executed.

Howard settled down in the screening room on Sunset Boulevard to indulge in an orgy of 'movie-screening'. He surrounded himself with a pile of junk food, confectionery and Kleenex boxes, compulsively arranging and rearranging the latter in geometric shapes on the table before him. He needed them to 'insulate' himself from the germ-ridden surfaces which, he believed, now hemmed him round.

He was careful to telephone Jean each evening with a progress report on his 'treatment', but having done so returned to his movies, often not stirring again for upwards of eighteen hours. After sitting in one position for many weeks, he arrived home with his haemorrhoids more acutely inflamed than ever. As he insisted on maintaining the fiction of the cure, he also robbed himself of the considerable pleasure of complaining about them.

By the mid 1950s, Howard's mental condition had deteriorated to the point that his senior aides were secretly considering having him declared insane. Hughes got wind of this and decided to furnish himself with an ally by marrying Jean Peters, whom he had been seeing on and off for the best part of ten years. They were married under assumed names in an obscure silver-mining town in the Nevada desert on 12th January 1957. Perhaps because of the difference in their ages – Jean was thirty, her husband fifty-one – they continued to maintain separate living quarters. It was not a close relationship and if Jean wished to talk to her husband she had first to contact a member of the Mormon Mafia to arrange an appointment.

On 30th June 1961, TWA filed an anti-trust complaint against Hughes in New York, complaining of mismanagement. He refused to testify and two years later a Federal court entered judgement by default, awarding the airline record damages of more than a hundred and forty-five million dollars. The case profoundly depressed Hughes and five months after its inception he moved with Jean to 1001 Bel-Air Road, Bel-Air. He retreated to one room at the top of this vast mansion where his growing fear of germs and pathological need to safeguard his privacy caused him to construct within its boundaries 'an enormously expensive and private asylum'. Although the *loci* were periodically to change, he was to remain its inmate for the rest of his life.

He now saw no one save his wife and the most trusted of his Mormon aides, whom he summoned not by a bell but by snapping his elongated finger-nails against a brown paper bag which he kept beside him to receive his discarded Kleenex. The windows of this meagre *lebensraum* were tightly curtained and sealed with masking tape. The carpet was never vacuumed, the furniture never dusted. The bed, which he seldom used, was rigidly aligned so that the feet exactly corresponded with pieces of masking tape fixed to the floor.*

Totally naked except for a tissue covering his loins, Howard spent his days watching an endless series of movies from a Barcalounge reclining chair 'insulated' with layers of Kleenex. His favourite was *Ice Station Zebra*, which he screened more than one hundred and fifty times. He knew the sound-track by heart. He was almost as fond of *The Blue Max*, *The Sting*, and *Butch Cassidy and the Sundance Kid*. He adored all the Bond films but preferred those made with Sean Connery. Romantic films he considered 'mushy'.

In his declining years, Howard Hughes became dependant on 'soft' drugs. In one twelve-hour period he ingested a hundred and seventy milligrams of Valium – sixty-eight times the recommended dose – and regularly injected himself with liquid codeine. As Bartlett and

*This may have been to frighten away evil spirits. For much the same reason another rich American, Cornelius Vanderbilt the Elder, is said to have kept a dish filled with salt under each leg of his bed.

Steele have pointed out, codeine dependence is an uncommon form of drug addiction. But then Howard Hughes was an uncommon man. 'As he had done in the movies and in aviation, he rewrote the medical record books on codeine abuse, pioneering a new form of addiction.' In the four years to 1970 his body absorbed the equivalent of thirty-three thousand codeine tablets; and when in 1976 surgeons at the Methodist Hospital in Houston came to perform a post-mortem on his body, they discovered fragments of hypodermic needles which had broken off in both arms years before.

His addiction caused him to eat only sparingly and with a child-like contrariness. He disliked large peas and employed a specially constructed rake through which only small ones could pass. The Poland spring water which he not only drank with every meal but employed for his self-administered enemas had to be served at exactly the right temperature; and the cubes of beef in his Irish stew had to be trimmed to an angle of exactly forty-five degrees. Howard inspected each cube personally before consuming it and any variation caused the dish to be returned to the kitchens.

For a time, he was also very fond of Swanson's TV Turkey Dinners – but would have preferred them to contain only white meat – and, for dessert, peach cobbler. One day he told an aide: 'Call the company and have them switch to peach cobbler and take out the dark meat'. The aide, who was relatively inexperienced in the ways of his employer, said: 'You're pulling my leg'.

Another of his short-lived attachments was to Baskin-Robbins' banana-and-nut-flavoured ice cream. For some months he ate a small scoopful with every meal. When it was noticed that stocks were running low, a domestic was sent out to acquire more. He returned empty-handed, reporting that the line had been discontinued. In a state of shock, the Mormon Mafia contacted Baskin-Robbins and begged them to make up a special batch. Although the minimum order was three hundred and fifty gallons, the purchase was authorised and the crisis averted. The very day the consignment arrived, Hughes announced that he no longer liked banana-and-nut-flavoured ice cream and would try a scoop of French vanilla instead. The Mormon aides spent the next twelve months asking everyone they knew whether they liked banana-and-nut-flavoured ice-cream. Those who said they did were presented with a two gallon drum.

Although it often took him eight hours to consume, Howard began each meal with a bowl of Campbell's chicken soup. He would take a spoonful and then grow preoccupied with the film he was watching. Noticing that the soup had grown cold, he would send it back to the kitchen to be reheated. This process was somctimes repeated fifteen or twenty times. When it was returned, and as he had a tendency to pick out all the lumps of chicken, he would complain that it was mostly broth. In time, the chef came to anticipate this grievance by opening a fresh tin, transferring the new chicken to the old soup and discarding the rest.

It was soon no longer enough that Howard should avoid the dread sting of an unseen germ himself – his staff must do likewise. When Bill Gay's wife was sufficiently incautious to develop a mild contagion, Howard banished her husband from his presence for fifteen years. Executives at Romaine Street were also instructed to limit their contact with outsiders; and when blue-collar workers dropped by to be paid, they were instructed to remain on the sidewalk. Their cheques were then floated down to them from a second-storey window. On windy days this created havoc both for the recipients and the hapless motorists trying to avoid them.

The Romaine Street staff were also forbidden to eat out, all meals consumed on duty being sent in from the kitchens of the Hughes Tool Company. Letters and parcels were collected from the postman by means of a bucket lowered on a rope and delivered in the same way.

To Hughes' mind, such precautions were essential. Danger lurked in the most unlikely quarters. One day a member of the Bel-Air domestic staff accidentally dropped a bottle on some stairs. The bottle shattered, littering the staircase with shards of glass. Having spent several hours pondering how best to deal with this problem, Howard instructed Romaine Street to send over a man equipped with a ruler and pencil to divide the affected area up into inch squares. These were then to be meticulously and individually brushed down and wiped clean.

In 1968, and in addition to his other oddities, Hughes developed an acute hypochondria. He was visited by one of his four physicians as often as six or seven times a day. The doctor was allowed neither to touch nor ask questions of his patient and his replies had to be written on a pad. As a result, one of the physicians suffered a nervous break down and ended his days an alcoholic.

Others learned from his example and escaped while there was still time. One of these was Hughes' barber, recruited in the late 1960s. He was paid a salary of five hundred dollars per week. In return for this he was expected to arrive at the Hughes residence not later than nine in the morning and remain until five in the evening. He passed his time reading comic-books and newspapers and solving crossword puzzles. He never once set eyes on his employer. Every day he asked one of the Mormon aides: 'Do you think Mr Hughes would like his hair cut today?' The answer never varied: 'Mr Hughes is all tied up today. Perhaps tomorrow'. Tomorrow never came and when the man could stand it no longer he contrived to get himself fired by demanding a two-hundred-percent increase in salary. Calculating that this was an extortionate rate for a non-haircut, Howard finally agreed to let go.

Only one barber ever got to cut Howard Hughes' hair. He found the experience so emotionally draining that he could never be persuaded to return. He was asked to bring thirty-six combs with him each of which had to be dipped into a special sterilising solution at every second stroke and discarded altogether after two minutes. Hughes kept his ears tightly folded down beneath his hands throughout the operation: 'so that none of that hair will get in me'.

For all these precautions, his standard of personal hygeine was often appalling. His fear of 'contaminated' surfaces meant that he could never bring himself to touch a door knob. When he wanted to use the toilet, he had to kick the bathroom door as a signal to one of his aides to come and open it. If the aide was slow in responding, Howard simply urinated on the floor. He would not allow the mess to be cleaned up, only absorbed by layers of Kleenex. None of the aides were permitted to use the bathroom whilst on duty and were instructed in case of emergency to relieve themselves in empty milk cartons.

In 1970, and after thirteen years of marriage, Jean Peters announced that she was divorcing her husband. Howard granted her an index-linked allowance of one hundred thousand dollars, payable for twenty years. Within two months of the decree being made absolute, Jean married the studio executive in charge of production at Twentieth Century Fox.

Rejected by his wife and terrified at the prospect of having to pay one hundred and forty-five million dollars in compensation to TWA, Hughes decided to leave America for ever. To this end 'the real and pitiful Wizard of Oz' devised the greatest of all his inventions: the travelling asylum. For the remaining six years of his life, and at a cost of ten million dollars, it was to carry him like some magic carpet from country to country in an endless search for peace and anonymity.

On 25th November 1970 he flew to Paradise Island in the Bahamas, taking up residence on the top floor of the Britannia Beach Hotel. Thirteen months later he became the focus of world-wide attention when the American publishing house of McGraw-Hill announced that it had acquired 'world publishing rights to a 230,000 word transcript of taped reminiscences of Howard R. Hughes' compiled by an obscure American writer named Clifford Irving.

The 'autobiography', which Irving had shown to McGraw-Hill did contain some authentic material, but nothing very new. The remainder was fictitious. Irving had never met Hughes. He had simply calculated that the same dislike of publicity which had caused the reclusive billionaire to refuse to testify in the TWA anti-trust case would prevent him coming forward now, to denounce the book.

He was wrong. After fifteen years of total seclusion, Hughes agreed to partake in a telephone link-up with a group of journalists who had known him in the old days. In measured tones he told them that he had never met Clifford Irving. 'I have never even heard of him until a matter of days ago when this thing first came to my attention.' Shortly afterwards, Irving admitted his book was a hoax. Sent to prison for his misdeeds, he passed the time by teaching Creative Writing.

During the telephone link-up, Hughes had scoffed at rumours of mandarin finger-nails and hair half way down his back and claimed that he would shortly abandon his reclusive lifestyle – 'I definitely expect to do it. I have intentions to do it'. But his was very far from the truth. The blinding publicity generated by the Irving affair had unsettled him; and thirty-nine days after the telephone interview he fled the Bahamas for the comparative seclusion of Nicaragua. After a brief sojourn in Canada, he returned to Nicaragua where, on 7th December 1972, he sold the Hughes Tool Company – the fount of all his wealth – for one hundred and fifty million dollars in order to secure his liability to TWA.

In the event, the sale need not have been made. Five weeks later, and in the twelfth year of the dispute, the Supreme Court overturned the judgement.

Some time around Christmas Eve 1972 – his sixty-seventh birthday – Howard arrived in London. He settled into a ninth floor penthouse at the Inn on the Park where, the following August, he suffered a bad fall, fracturing his hip. He was taken to hospital to have it set. The anaesthetist who presided over the operation described his patient as 'much older than his sixty-seven years' and 'extremely emaciated'. He feared that the billionaire's teeth which were loose 'and in a very poor state' might, during surgery, work free 'and be aspirated into [his] lung'.

The fear proved groundless. A pin was inserted into the hip and the operation was an unqualified success. Howard should have made a steady and full recovery. But he was no ordinary patient. He refused to undertake the prescribed exercises and in consequence remained bed-ridden for the remaining two and a half years of his life.

Five days before Christmas 1973, the Mormon Mafia spirited its employer back to the Bahamas and installed him in the Xanadu Princess Hotel. He was now eating nothing, drawing febrile nourishment only from an intake of codeine which would have killed ten ordinary men. In February 1976, and for reasons which have never been clearly determined, his aides falsely represented that Bahamian supplies of the drug codeine were almost exhausted and flew him on the last complete journey of his life – to a *sanctum sanctorum* atop the Princess Hotel in Acapulco, Mexico. He would occupy it for just fifty-five days.

The years of self-neglect had taken their toll and 'the most powerful, curious and fascinating American of his age' was now no more than a semi-derelict ruin. His six-foot four-inch frame had shrunk by three inches and he weighed less than ninety-three pounds. He had an open tumour on his forehead. His finger-nails and toe-nails had grown to above two inches and had curled back on themselves like a jester's slippers. His hair was matted and whispy. His back consumed by bed sores.

When the Mormon Mafia – which had so long pandered without question or query to its master's phobias and obsessions – took the unprecedented step of approving lifetime contracts for itself, it was evident that the end could not be long delayed. Like the concentration-camp commandants of old, they would later claim that they could not be held responsible – had only been following orders. The truth is less palatable. Drawn from the ranks of semi-literate truck drivers, used-car salesmen and hawkers of life assurance – who in any business empire save the topsy-turvey one of Howard Hughes would have been relegated to the role of tea-maker and office boy – they had become the grateful and willing stooges of their master's bizarre fantasies, sacrificing their much-bruted religious and moral beliefs on the altar of expediency. In exchange for a lavish lifestyle and financial security they had not only bowed down to his madness, they had nurtured and manipulated it to their own ends.

On Saturday 3rd April 1976 a doctor was called to the Acapulco Princess Hotel where he found Hughes lying on his bed, twitching compulsively. He diagnosed uraemic poisoning, a form of kidney failure. (A subsequent post-mortem was to show that due to codeine abuse Hughes' kidneys were less than half the normal weight and size.) Shortly afterwards he passed into a coma. The moment which his aides had dreaded had finally arrived – the moment he would have to be flown back to America for treatment.

The seventy-year-old billionaire was placed in an ambulance which raced with sirens blaring to the airport. Here he was loaded aboard an aircraft which had been chartered to take him to the Methodist Hospital in Houston, Texas – the city of his birth which he had left thirty-eight years earlier after his triumphal flight around the world. At 1.27 on the afternoon of 5th April 1976, as the plane passed over the Rio Grande, he died – just thirty minutes away from the hospital which might have prolonged his life.

Two days later, encased in an eight-thousand-dollar coffin, he was laid to rest beside his mother and father in Glenwood Cemetery. Sixteen mourners attended the eight-minute graveside ceremony and there was not a wet eye in the house. Howard Hughes was now very literally in death what he had always been in life: a puzzle within an enigma . . . sealed in a box.

Although he left holdings and cash worth in excess of three billion dollars, he died intestate. A number of people came forward to claim his fortune, including a compulsive quiz-show contestant named Melvin Dummer, who alleged that he had given a lift and lent a quarter to a man purporting to be Hughes, who in gratitude agreed to leave him one-sixteenth of his estate. Some three dozen wills have currently been filed for probate. No one claim has been established beyond any other and it seems likely that the bulk of his fortune will pass either to the twenty-one distant relatives to whom he never spoke, or be absorbed into the national exchequer – to which, in life, he contributed so little.

Chapter 6

Funny Peculiar. Funny Ha Ha

In 1908 the American Harry Bensley was a personable young playboy. His clothes were the best that money could buy and he was always to be seen in the most fashionable Mayfair nightspots. He was popular with his 'set' and he knew how to enjoy himself. He was not at all the stuff of which eccentrics are made.

Two other men who fancied that they knew how to enjoy themselves during the Edwardian era were the American banker John Pierpont Morgan and Lord Lonsdale. They were both enormously rich and enjoyed indulging in outlandish wagers. One day Morgan bet Lord Lonsdale that he could not procure a man willing to travel around the world without once showing his face. In doing so he changed the course of Harry Bensley's life.

When nobody came forward to accept the challenge it was supposed that his Lordship would be forced to concede defeat. Much to his friends' surprise, Harry Bensley volunteered. When he heard the conditions of the wager he wished he had not. He would be required to wear an iron mask weighing four and a half pounds; and with the exception of twenty shillings sterling, and one change of underwear, would be permitted to take nothing with him. He would be allowed to finance himself only by the sale of postcards. In the course of his journeyings he would have to pass through numerous English towns and villages as well as one hundred and twenty-five towns in eighteen other countries. He would also be expected to find himself a wife. How he was to do this without showing his face was not explained.

The adventure began well. Pushing a pram – a last minute

concession – he set off for Newmarket races where he sold Edward VII a postcard for £5. In a state of heady euphoria he then tramped on to Beckley Heath – where he was arrested as a vagrant. On being brought before the magistrates he was ordered to remove his mask. When he explained that to do so would nullify the wager, the magistrates relented and he was charged as 'The Man in the Iron Mask'. He was fined half-a-crown.

It would be amusing to chronicle his adventures over the next six years as he wandered through twelve countries. Unfortunately, they were rather prosaic. In 1914 and with great reluctance, Harry abandoned the quest in order to volunteer for the army. Lord Lonsdale sportingly presented him with a consolation prize of £4,000 which Harry donated to charity. Although he never admitted as much, he lived to regret it. Three years later, with the coming of the Bolshevik revolution, his private fortune evaporated and he spent the rest of his life a relatively poor man, dying largely forgotten by his old Mayfair cronies in a seaside boarding house in 1956.

Mayfair was also the home for many years of the eccentric Marquis of Salisbury, Conservative prime minister to Queen Victoria in succession to Disraeli. Blessed with the gift of true self-possession, he was always destined to do well in politics from the moment when, in the course of delivering his maiden speech, he paused to yawn. Disraeli turned to a colleague and muttered: 'He'll do'. He had a great love of animals and his constant companion was a huge boar-hound called 'Pharaoh' – from its reluctance to let people go.

In addition to his home in Arlington Street, Lord Salisbury owned Hatfield House, an Elizabethan mansion in Hertfordshire. In order to maintain a uniform impression, the library door was fitted with shelves of artificial books. When closed, these dovetailed so cunningly with their companions that on one occasion the Marquis and a friend spent the best part of an hour trying to find their way out. They eventually had to admit defeat and ring for a servant to release them.

At the age of seventy, Lord Salisbury took up tricycling and became a familiar sight about the roads of Hatfield. A servant accompanied him on these jaunts, assisting on the steeper hills with a push in the back. Faced with the descent, he got up behind, his feet straddling the axle, and coasted down with his hands resting on his master's shoulders.

When the Marquis was just four years old, his ancestor – the Marchioness of Salisbury, known familiarly as 'Old Sarum' – died at Hatfield House. Although she ruled smart society from Arlington Street for more than half a century, 'Old Sarum' secretly preferred the pursuits of the country and for forty-four years was mistress of the Hatfield Hounds. In 1819 old age forced her to relinquish this office, but nothing could persuade her to forego the pleasures of the chase entirely. Lashed to her horse, she was led to each fence where, at the critical moment, her groom would shout: 'Damn you, my lady, jump!' She had almost no knowledge of the scriptures and seldom went to church. When she did she caused nothing but embarrassment. On one occasion, listening to a sermon on the Fall of Man and hearing that Adam had excused himself by saying 'Lord, the woman tempted me', she shook her head in a very violent manner and muttered: 'Shabby fellow, indeed'. She died at Hatfield House in 1834 in a suitably eccentric manner. The ubiquitous Samuel Rogers quit the house on:

> The very morning the catastrophe occurred. I then shook her by the hand – that hand which was soon to be a cinder. In the evening, after she had been dressed for dinner, her maid left her to go to tea.

> She was then writing letters; and it is supposed that, having stooped down her head – she was very short-sighted – the flame of the candle caught her head-dress.

Eighty years later, the newspaper magnate Lord Northcliffe met an equally bizarre end in a wooden hut atop a house belonging to the Duke of Devonshire. When he no longer quite knew what he was about, he is said to have stumbled from his eerie and telephoned the editor of one of his newspapers. 'There is a story going the rounds that I'm mad' said he. 'I hope we're covering it.'

In a sense, Northcliffe had been mad all his life. During the Great War he became convinced that the Germans were plotting his assassination; he also suspected that he was the reincarnation of Napoleon Bonaparte, a crotchet so common as to be almost banal. When he tried on the little Corsican's hat, suspicion hardened into certainty: it was a perfect fit. His delusions were consistently reinforced by his staff, who naturally wished to remain on good terms with him. As he was an unpredictable employer, this was far from easy. When the portly figure of the boss was seen roaming the corridors of Carmelite House, men of sense made themselves scarce. Those who did not might be carried off to an expensive lunch. They also ran the risk of being ordered to report to his office. Having done so, they would be shown into an ante-room where they would kick their heels for several hours whilst a succession of aides and secretaries rushed in and out whispering conflicting rumours. When Northcliffe grew tired of maintaining the charade, he would emerge from his inner sanctum and tell the poor dupe that there had been a mistake, that he was not required. Most of his employees accepted these occasional alarms as an occupational hazard. To some extent everyone who worked for Northcliffe lived in the shadow of the boot.

It would be wrong to suggest, however, that 'the Napoleon of Fleet Street' was in all things bad. The short-tempered bully who trampled on unwelcome callers' hats also had his human side. He adored children and was capable of quite incredible generosity. He knew how to be kind and his several brothers all shared in his prosperity. His love for his mother, who outlived him, never diminished.

His last illness came upon him whilst travelling in Europe. Having stopped to make a purchase from an ice cream vendor, he formed the idea that the man was a spy and his merchandise poisoned. He was returned to England in a strait-jacket, accompanied by two burly 'attendants.' His newspapers announced that he was suffering from 'a disordered appendix'.

Among Lord Northcliffe's many bugaboos, two stand supreme: his hatred of Americans and his private dislike of inherited wealth. He would have despised Lord Astor who qualified on both counts. At one time, Lord Astor owned the largest private residence ever to grace the Victorian Embankment. He was very friendly with Daisy, the beautiful Countess of Warwick, and one day invited her to step down and view the contents of what he described as his 'treasure room'. Thinking that he meant to show her a collection of silver, perhaps an old master or two, she descended deep into the bowels of the earth and entered a steel-lined vault. Here she found herself confronted by rows of wooden shelves stacked high with bags of gold. Lord Astor said that these represented the accumulation of many years. He was convinced that England would shortly be plunged into revolution. When that day came, he and his hoard would quietly slip away by boat to France.

The revolution, of course, never came. But as the years ticked by, Lord Astor's insecurities multiplied. Like Northcliffe, he lived in dread of assassination and spent much of his time in reclusive retreat at Hever Castle, once the home of Anne Boleyn. Guests occupied cottages in the grounds and were required to return to them directly after dinner. The multi-millionaire then bolted himself into his stronghold and the door was not unlocked under any pretext until the following morning.

An altogether more robust type of eccentric was Squire Osbaldestone who in a long life came close to embodying the spirit of perpetual motion. He regularly fought men twice his size, played billiards for fifty hours continuously, killed a hundred pheasants with as many shots, defeated the French tennis champion using only his hand as a racquet, and saved an important cricket match by bowling in a drunken stupor whilst suffering from a broken shoulder. Physical pain meant nothing to him. On one occasion, while out with the guns, he was accidentally shot in the eye but refused to complain for fear of curtailing the day's sport. He was exceptionally gallant and thought nothing of riding fifty miles to fetch a flower for a young lady's ballgown. He adored horses and once undertook to gallop two hundred miles at an average speed of twenty-four miles an hour. Although this was thought to be impossible, he triumphed with time to spare, having changed horses no less than sixty-three times. He married at the ripe age of sixty-five and was shortly afterwards faced with the greatest challenge of his life – to sit in a chair for twenty-four hours without stirring. He won the bet, but not without difficulty. Having entirely dissipated his fortune, he existed in old age on the daily sovereign doled out by his wife.

Another figure on the borderland of fable was the Earl of Peterborough, the last of the knights-errant. On one occasion he dressed as a young woman and kept an assignation with the infamous Judge Jeffreys in order to protect his sweetheart from the Hanging Judge's unwelcome advances. He had an excess of high spirits and once prodded a dandy – to whom he had taken an instant and irrational dislike – halfway down the Strand at sword-point.

Like many young bloods, he fancied himself a lover and posed for some months as a miller's apprentice in order to win the heart of his daughter. When another of his affairs began to pall, he secretly visited the husband and presented him with five hundred pounds on the condition that he take the lady back.

Peterborough is sometimes said to have been the first man of rank to marry an actress. Although he kept the union a secret for thirteen years, he was exceptionally fond of his wife and when she was jeered at he leapt on to the stage and administered a thrashing on her leading man. As he grew older he became increasingly domesticated and was often to be seen wandering around the markets looking for a chicken and a cauliflower tricked out in the Order of the Garter. Whether he really encompassed the marvellous feats attributed to him, or was merely 'the ramblingest lying rogue on earth', will never now be known. A few hours after he died – 'of a Flux of eating Grapes' – his wife threw his three-volume autobiography into the fire.

A more certain hero was that 'brave rough English Admiral', Sir Cloudesley Shovel. Although he was born poor, Shovel quickly rose to command as the result of several spectacular feats of bravery. One of these entailed swimming round the Fleet during engagements carrying messages in his teeth.

After a long and distinguished career, he met his death in a very curious way. In 1707, after an inconclusive engagement off Toulon, he was returning with the Fleet to England when his ship, *HMS Association*, ran into a thick fog off the Scilly Isles. In a very forthright manner, one of his sailors warned him that he was in danger of running aground. Sir Cloudesley, fearing a mutiny, had the man hanged from the yard-arm. He went to his death reciting verses from the Bible. Moments later, the ship struck a rock and sank. As a result, and from that day to this, sailors have been loath to quote directly from the Bible during a burial at sea.

When Shovel's body was found washed ashore, it was naturally assumed that he had drowned. A quarter of a century later, however, the wife of a local fisherman confessed on her death-bed that she had found the Admiral lying unconscious on some rocks and had smothered him for the sake of a valuable ring. The woman gave the ring to the priest who heard her confession and after her death it was forwarded to Shovel's old friend, the Earl of Berkeley, in the possession of whose descendants it still remains. His sterling qualities earned Shovel a last resting place at Westminster Abbey and a number of fulsome epitaphs. One of the most precious begins:

> In sable weeds let widowed Albion mourn,
> And dismal pomp her shining cliffs adorn,
> Let want of Light on her once glorious shore,
> In mourning tell: Great Shovel is no more.

There was also the grief of his sovereign, Queen Anne:

> His royal Mrs, too, mourns o'er his grave,
> She knew him useful as she knew him brave.

Equally useful to his royal Mrs was William Ewart Gladstone, four times prime minister to Queen Victoria. His greatness may have been due, at least in part, to the fact that he needed so little sleep. It was his practice to take a stone hot-water bottle to bed with him, filled with tea. As he seldom slept more than four hours, this was still warm enough to drink when he awoke. From an early age he trained himself to drop a mental curtain on the cares of the day as soon as he got into bed. In this way he was able to fall asleep almost immediately. The trick only failed him once: having half cut through a tree on his brother-in-law's estate, he lay awake all night worrying whether the thunderstorm then raging would bring it crashing through the roof.

A frenzied, compulsive sort of man, he developed some curious fixations. He believed that it was only possible to guarantee a long life by chewing each mouthful of food exactly thirty-two times; and once held forth for half an hour on the contrasting merits of boiled and poached eggs. His erudition was formidable and a constant source of irritation to others. One evening, a group of his colleagues resolved to be revenged and having boned up on the art of ancient Chinese music – a subject of which they were certain Gladstone knew nothing – proceeded over dinner to monopolise the conversation. The Grand Old Man listened for some time in silence, then with a look of dawning comprehension, said: 'You have evidently been reading an article I wrote some ten years ago. But since then I have studied the matter afresh and have conversed with well-informed travellers and I have arrived at directly opposite conclusions . . .' He then proceeded to demolish his former theories utterly. He did so in his inimitable manner, punctuating his remarks with a series of curious body contortions and generally bending and stretching and wriggling about in the manner of one possessed.

Lloyd George thought Gladstone more than a little mad and said that he had 'terrifying eyes'. Disraeli believed that he was 'intoxicated with his own verbosity'. His smugness and sense of superiority led another politician to remark: 'I have no objection to Mr Gladstone having an ace up his sleeve – only to his unshakeable belief that God put it there.'

In his spare time, Gladstone tramped the streets of London in an endeavour to redeem fallen women. Suitable candidates were taken home to meet his wife who, if we are to believe Lady Augusta Fane, was more than a little eccentric herself. On one occasion she was observed leaving a supper party in obvious discomfort. It later transpired that she had stuffed several ham sandwiches down the front of her evening dress – sandwiches heavily laced with mustard.

Gladstone's desk at Eton is still preserved, the last letters of his name, which he cut in the top, squashed up concertina-fashion. It stands as a memorial not only to the man, but to the only project which he ever undertook without allowing himself sufficient room to manoeuvre.

During his time at Eton, Gladstone acquired a love of walking which was to remain with him all his life. In later years, during his visits to Queen Victoria at Balmoral, he regularly set off across the moors at dawn, returning at dusk having covered more than thirty miles. Walking was then considered rather a fashionable recreation for gentlemen and another prime minister much addicted to it was Sir Henry Campbell-Bannerman. 'A bon-vivant, a boulevardier and a humorist', it was his habit before going out to talk very quietly to his collection of walking-sticks, soothing with fulsome phrases all but the one selected.

This habit of investing inanimate objects with human characteristics and qualities is curiously widespread. Yet those most vulnerable to it are often in other respects quite unsentimental. This was certainly true of the ruffianly Thomas Pitt, the last Lord Camelford, a notorious eighteenth-century duellist, who was rumoured to have bestowed pet names on each of his pistols. His house was a veritable armoury and 'strongly expressive of the pugnacity of the peer'. Pride of place was given to 'a long thick bludgeon . . . horizontally supported by two brass hooks. Above this was placed parallel one of lesser dimensions, until a pyramid of weapons gradually arose, tapering to a horsewhip'.

For all his violent propensities, Lord Camelford was not entirely bad. He was generous to a fault, a reliable friend and a stout champion of the poor and needy. One day, driving with a lady companion, he came to a turnpike where he paid the toll and received his change in halfpennies. Having gone a short distance beyond the toll, he suddenly reined in the horses, examined the coins he had been given, jumped down and ran back. His companion saw him grab the toll-keeper by the throat and throw him to the ground. He then quietly returned to the carriage, where he said: 'I dare say you thought I was going to put myself in a passion. But these rascals have barrels of bad halfpennies which they give in change to the people who pass through the gates. To you and me it does not signify, but to the poor it does. Some poor carter perhaps has nothing but his change to pay for his supper and when he gets to his journey's end, he finds he can't get his bread and cheese'.

A nephew of the great Earl of Chatham, Camelford was born at Bocinnoc in Cornwall in February 1775. At fourteen he entered the royal navy as a midshipman but proved so refractory and disobedient that Captain Vancouver, who had charge of him aboard the *Discovery*, had to discipline him. Shortly after succeeding to his father's title and estates, young Tom encountered the captain in London and was only prevented from striking him on the intervention of a brother officer. The incident played upon Vancouver's mind and he died shortly afterwards.

In 1797, at the age of twenty-two, Camelford was appointed to the command of a sloop named the *Favourite* then lying at English Harbour, Antigua. Due to the absence of his senior officer on naval business at St Kitts, he found himself temporarily in command of the station and at some point issued an order to Lieutenant Charles Peterson, who in his captain's absence, was in charge of the flagship. Mr Petersen ignored Lord Camelford's instructions on the grounds that his authority did not extend to the vessel of a superior officer. A row developed and Peterson, who seems to have been as hot-headed as Lord Camelford, confronted his Lordship at the head of a band of armed sailors. Lord Camelford at once drew up his own men and brandishing a pistol, walked close up to the Lieutenant. He said: 'Do you still persist in disobeying my orders?' Mr Petersen, who had formerly served aboard the *Favourite* and had been passed over for promotion in favour of Lord Camelford, replied: 'Yes, I do persist'. Lord Camelford, who suffered from an acute inferiority complex which constantly forced him to prove to himself that he was not a coward, shot Mr Petersen dead.

At a court-martial held aboard the *Invincible* at Martinique, he was honourably acquitted of the murder on the grounds that he had done no more than was necessary to quell an armed mutiny. Nonetheless he shortly afterwards left the navy. He next formed an insane scheme to render his country a service by going secretly to Paris 'and in the midst of their capital attack the rulers of that hostile country'. Fortunately for his own safety, the plot was disclosed before it could be put into commission.

Deprived of this last useful channel for his fiery energies, Lord Camelford degenerated into a lout. When an old gentleman at Drury Lane theatre expressed a mild wish to look into the auditorium through a glass viewing panel which his Lordship was obstructing, Camelford knocked him down a flight of stairs and beat him so severely that he all but lost the use of an eye. The gentleman sued him before Lord Kenyon and was awarded five hundred pounds damages.

Together with his friend, Captain Barrie, he next attempted to chastise the nightwatchmen in Cavendish Square. A pitched battle ensued and at the end of an hour the two young bloods were overpowered and carried to the compter by twenty members of the watch.

In 1801, when peace was declared, Lord Camelford, who openly mourned the end of hostilities, refused to put a candle in his window as a sign of rejoicing. In consequence, his house was attacked by the mob. Lifting down his cudgel from the base of the pyramid, he sallied forth and began to lay about him. The odds against him were overwhelming and he received a terrible beating. The next day he hired a band of ruffianly seamen and secreted them in his house in case the mob should return. It didn't.

'A well-looking man but with rather a slang manner', Lord Camelford went each day to the Prince of Wales coffee-house in Conduit Street for the purpose of reading the newspapers. Given his hair-trigger temper and irritable disposition, he was usually left to do so in peace. But one night a first-rate blood crashed down beside him and called very loudly for a glass of port. He then looked round with a great air of boredom, picked up a broadsheet . . . and purloined Lord Camelford's candle by which to read it. When his drink arrived, he took the candle off with him to the other side of the room.

Lord Camelford sat for a while lapped in what – from experience – the waiters knew to be a mood of dangerous abstraction. Then, mimicking the young man's voice, he called for a pair of snuffers, crossed the room and extinguished the offending flame. Growing indignant, the young aristocrat called to the waiter: 'Who the devil is this fellow who dares to insult a gentleman? What is he? What do they call him?' When he was told, he started up, trembling violently. He flung down some money and hurried out into the night, leaving his drink untouched.

In 1804, at the age of twenty-nine, Lord Camelford had another altercation in the Prince of Wales coffee-house – this time with his good friend, Captain Best. The dispute arose when a companion, thinking to compliment him, described his Lordship as 'the second finest shot in England'. Camelford (who had imagined himself unparalleled) demanded the name of his superior. His companion said: 'Why, Captain Best, to be sure'.

It was a slender enough pretext for a feud, but the two men resolved to settle the matter in a field south-west of Holland House, now the site of Melbury Road. The night before the encounter, Lord Camelford quietly sat down and made his will. He freely confessed that the quarrel was unjust and that 'if I should lose my life in a contest of my own seeking, I most solemnly forbid any of my friends or relations . . . from instituting any vexatious proceedings against my protagonist'. Duelling being forbidden by law, he also requested that if Captain Best should be proceeded against for his part in the matter, 'this part of my will may be made known to the King, in order that his royal heart may be moved to extend his mercy towards him'.

Shortly after dawn on Wednesday 7th March 1804, the two protagonists came face to face. Captain Best made one more attempt to make his friend see reason. With a gesture of impatience, and pricked on by fate, Lord Camelford said: 'Best, this is child's play. The thing must go on'. The distance was fixed at a murderously short thirty paces. When it was discovered that Tom Camelford was to fire first, nobody gave Captain Best much chance of escaping with his life.

Against all the odds, Lord Camelford missed. It was whispered that his opponent would now make a gallant end to the matter and discharge his pistol into the air. After this the two men could be decently reconciled. Instead, Captain Best took careful aim and shot his friend through the body. Lord Camelford pitched forward at full length, mortally wounded.

The sound of gunfire had attracted a group of Lord Holland's gardeners who now ran up in an attempt to prevent Captain Best leaving the field. Lord Camelford said: 'I do not wish him to be stopped. I freely forgive him and I hope God will forgive him too'.

He was carried to Little Holland House where he continued in agonies of pain for three days. He said that 'he had never really felt any ill-will towards any man' and was at a loss to explain his pugnacious behaviour. Towards half-past eight on the Saturday evening, he died.

In his will he left a fortune of £150,000 and a request that his body be taken to the shores of Lake St Pierre, at Berne. Here would be found three trees. The centre one of these was to be removed, his body put into the ground and the tree replaced. In consideration of their compliance with his wishes, he left the landowners a bequest of one thousand pounds. He added: 'At the foot of this tree I formerly passed many hours in solitude contemplating the mutability of human affairs'.

Until such time as these instructions could be carried out, his body was wrapped in a lead coffin and lodged in the crypt of St Anne's, Soho. When the time came for its removal, it was found to have disappeared, stolen in all probability by the Resurrection Men who made a living by selling corpses to the surgeons for dissection. Human affairs are very mutable.

The last hope of solving the mystery disappeared when the church of St Anne's was destroyed by enemy action during the Blitz. All that now remains is the tower. On the western side of this is a plaque, erected at the expense of the memoirist, Horace Walpole. It commemorates an even greater eccentric than Lord Camelford: Theodore, King of Corsica.

A Prussian adventurer and mercenary, Theodore was 'elected' King of Corsica in 1736 after leading a successful rebellion against the Genoese. For the first seven months of his 'reign' he financed his tiny kingdom by the sale of knighthoods. When this source of revenue dried up, he set out to raise funds in England. For some not quite certain reason he was refused permission to re-enter Corsica and, after two abortive attempts to regain his throne, settled in London. In 1756 he was imprisoned for a debt of five hundred pounds. His release was secured partly by a subscription raised by Horace Walpole and partly, as the plaque on the church tower attests, by registering 'his kingdom of Corsica for the use of his creditors'. Soon after his release, friendless and without a penny to his name, he died. As Horace Walpole wrote:

> Fate pour'd its lessons on his living head,
> Bestow'd a kingdom and denied him bread.

The cost of his funeral was defrayed by a local tradesman John Wright, who said: 'I am willing *for once* to pay the funeral expenses of a king'.

Theodore is commemorated by a public house in nearby Kemp's Court and by a brewery, which named a type of brandy after him. His family inherited his ill-luck. Depressed by money troubles, his son shot himself in the churchyard of St Margaret's, the pretty little church which nestles in the lea of Westminster Abbey; and his granddaughter was Mary Anne Clarke.

Known to history as the mistress of 'the Grand Old Duke of York', Mary Anne was born at Oxford, twenty years after her grandfather's death. Harold Dearden relates that by the time she was seventeen she was blessed with 'a distressingly feminine figure' and the kind of 'tip-tilted nose . . . which has proved the downfall of incautious males from time immemorial'.

In due course she married the younger but unstable son of a well-to-do builder. Unfortunately, her husband's extravagant way of life soon brought him to the brink of ruin. When he abandoned her, Mary Anne placed her children with relatives and resolved to provide for them by utilising her beauty to attract a wealthy lover. This scheme rather rebounded on her.

In 1803, at Brighton, Mary Anne met Frederick Augustus, Duke of York, the second son of George III and brother to the Prince Regent. He was then forty years of age and possessed an income of seventy thousand pounds a year. He had the reputation of a hardened drinker who regularly consumed seven bottles of claret with his dinner. He was also the prisoner of a loveless marriage to a Prussian Princess, a restless unfulfilled woman who seldom slept more than two or three hours and whiled away the rest of the night by roaming through her husband's Pall Mall mansion, reading aloud to herself. She owned forty dogs, several parrots and a monkey. A great patron of the arts, she was the first person of rank to encourage a little-known

Frenchwoman named Marie Tussaud. In later life, when she had become estranged from her husband and had no other company than the inmates of her menagerie, she rather pathetically commissioned Marie to fashion an effigy in wax of a sleeping baby.

In direct contrast to his wife, the Duke of York, says Thackeray, was 'a man, big, burly, loud, jolly, cursing, courageous'. Known as 'the soldiers' friend', he was also Commander-in-Chief of the British army. An enlightened general, he instituted a number of thoroughgoing reforms without which, twenty years later, the battle of Waterloo would almost certainly have been lost. He nonetheless had a tendency to vacillate in the field; and the somewhat contradictory orders issued by him in Flanders, when still young and comparatively inexperienced, gave rise to the famous jingle. Whether he ever really marched ten thousand men to the top of a hill and down again may be open to doubt.

Life under the patronage of the Duke of York was more luxurious than anything Mary Anne had ever known. She maintained two establishments, one in Gloucester Place, the other at Weybridge. According to Harold Dearden: 'Frederick Augustus confused the matter of engaging his household staff with the recruiting of a battalion' and she had 'no less than twenty-five servants to look after her, including two butlers, six footmen and three or four chefs who came in daily at a guinea a head'. Food was ordered in vast quantities and consumed at a terrible pace. Unfortunately, it was not paid for quite so promptly. Frederick Augustus was notoriously spendthrift and his lack of money was a byword. It followed him to the grave and it followed him beyond it. Seven years after his death, every soldier in the British army was ordered to 'donate' one day's pay towards the commission of a statue to their former Commander-in-Chief. On completion, it was placed one hundred and twenty-four feet in the air atop a Tuscan column in Waterloo Place. This led to the wits to joke that his lofty situation had been devised to enable him to escape his creditors; and that the rather undignified lightning conductor issuing from the top of his head was a spike on which to deposit unpaid bills.

The Duke and Mary Anne had not been lovers for very long before the baying of the Duke's creditors became a source of serious embarrassment to her. It was not simply that the Duke lacked the means to pay them; he failed to understand the necessity. Being an honourable girl who hated to owe money to anybody, Mary Anne decided that she would have to solve the problem herself. She found a source of previously untapped income immediately to hand.

The sale of army commissions, whilst strictly unofficial, was nevertheless an established fact of eighteenth century military life. The Hanoverians were forever casting nervous glances in the direction of the exiled Stuarts, on the other side of the Channel, and with 'kings more or less being tried on as if they were hats', it was generally agreed that the status quo could only be maintained by investing power in those least likely to benefit from a revolution: the landed aristocracy. The revenue from the sale of commissions also went some way towards defraying the cost of maintaining a standing army. As the years went by and those costs increased, the 'fees' likewise escalated. In Mary Anne's day a lieutenant-colonelcy in the foot guards could be had for seven thousand pounds. A hundred years later, when such perks were openly sold at auction, that price had almost doubled.

With the Duke's influence at her command, Mary Anne began touting for custom. Business was soon very brisk and she kept a list of prospective clients pinned to the curtain of her bed. For all this, her personal profit was negligible: nearly all the money went to pay her lover's debts.

It would all have been worthwhile if Frederick Augustus had only cared for her. But he did not; and when he tired of the relationship he sent his agent to inform her that he never wished to see her again. Despite the base and brutal manner of her dismissal, Mary Anne acquiesced, asking only that the Duke allow her a pension of four hundred pounds a year on which to maintain herself and her children. As this represented very little more than half of one percent of his yearly income it was not an unreasonable demand. Yet his extravagance was such that within the space of twelve months he was forced to stop paying.

Unable to meet her debts – most of which had been incurred on behalf of her blackguardly lover prior to their estrangement – Mary Anne was now in very real danger of being sent to prison. In a moment of desperation, she threatened to write her memoirs. Hearing of this, the Duke's political enemies raised certain questions in the House of Commons in the hope of discrediting him. Mary Anne was called to attest to the truth of her allegations. She gave her evidence in such a dignified and subdued manner that Frederick Augustus was removed from office and charged with corrupt practices. None of this, of course, materially altered Mary Anne's situation. She continued to be very desperate for money and again approached her former lover in the hope of obtaining common justice in the matter of her debts. At first Frederick Augustus repeated that he could do nothing. But when she renewed her threat to write her reminiscences he ceased to plead poverty, restored her forthwith to her pension and settled her outstanding liabilities.

Armed with this annuity, Mary Anne left England for ever. A year later, Frederick Augustus was reinstated as Commander-in-Chief of the army and all charges against him were dropped. Mary Anne settled at Boulogne. She died there in 1852 at the age of seventy-six, having outlived her royal lover by a quarter of a century. The Duke died in January 1827 and was buried at Windsor where he seems to have exerted a malign influence to the last. On the evening of his funeral St George's Chapel was so damp that at least two senior churchmen contracted fatal chills.

In some respects the first half of the nineteenth century represents the *belle epoque* of bizarre and eccentric funerals. When 'the English Sternutophile', Mrs Margaret Thompson, died at her house in Boyle Street, Mayfair, she left instructions that she be laid in a coffin packed with:

> all my handkerchiefs that I may have unwashed at the time of my decease . . . together with such a quantity of the best Scotch snuff (in which . . . I always had the greatest delight) as will cover my deceased body.

She requested for her funeral:

> Six men to be my bearers, who are known to be the greatest snuff-takers in the parish of St. James's, Westminster; instead of mourning, each to wear a snuff-coloured beaver hat which I desire be bought for that purpose and given to them. Six maidens of my old acquaintance, to bear my pall, each to wear a proper hood, and to carry a box filled with the best Scotch snuff to take for their refreshment as they go along. Before my corpse, I desire the

> minister may be invited to walk and to take a certain quantity of the said snuff, not exceeding one pound, to whom also I bequeath five guineas on condition of his so doing. And I also desire my old and faithful servant, Sarah Stuart, to walk before the corpse, to distribute every twenty yards a large handful of Scotch snuff to the ground and upon the crowd who may possibly follow me to the burial place; on which condition I bequeath her twenty pounds. And I also desire that at least two bushels of the said snuff may be distributed at the door of my house in Boyle Street.

A third bizarre funeral of the period was that of Lady Hester Stanhope, niece to William Pitt and cousin of the pugnacious Lord Camelford. The eldest of three daughters, she was born at Chevening, in Kent, in 1776. Her mother was William Pitt's sister, her father a dedicated republican. Considering his coaches to be an unwarranted symbol of aristocratic privilege he firstly erased the coat-of-arms from the doors and ultimately sold them, going about on foot like other people did. Hester took exception to this and acquired a pair of stilts, ostensibly to 'protect her petticoats from the mud', but in fact to shame her father into replacing them. Her father, however, remained fixed in his ideas and after the French revolution took to calling himself 'Citizen Stanhope'. During the Napoleonic wars he attracted considerable suspicion in government quarters and there was some talk of prosecuting him for High Treason as a French spy.

Beautiful, dominant and wilful, Lady Hester hated her family and could hardly wait to be out of it. On a trip to Hastings, she slipped away while her governess's back was turned and commandeered a small boat in the hope of rowing to France. As punishment for this grand idiocy she was set to mind the turkeys on the common.

After her coming-out ball, at which she made many enemies by behaving with lofty insolence, she scandalised society by forming an attachment to her boisterous cousin, Lord Camelford, going with him everywhere without a chaperone. Had he lived, she might have married him. In the event, the year before his death, she was invited by her uncle, the prime minister, to become his housekeeper. She accepted with alacrity. Her father, who detested his brother-in-law's policies, instantly disinherited her. Mindful of this, when Pitt died in 1806 he left her an annuity of £1500 per annum.

This was all the money she then had in the world. But she decided to quit England and in 1810 set sail aboard the frigate *Jason*. The ship was wrecked in the Aegean, but Lady Hester survived unscathed.

Recalling the prophecy of a Bedlam lunatic that she would one day be crowned Queen of the East, she now hurried on to Jerusalem where her wonderful complexion, flashing eyes and imperious manner captivated the locals who had seen nothing like her. A few years later she established herself at Acre. The local Pasha, who was as fascinated by her as everyone else, presented her with a semi-derelict convent at Dahar-Jûne and this she turned into a palace of such splendour that within ten years it was rumoured to exceed anything in Lebanon. In those days and in the East, it was possible to accomplish a great deal on fifteen hundred per annum.

In the fullness of time, Hester adopted eastern ways entirely. She also became something of an object of pilgrimage. She had a vain attachment to her high arches, beneath which, she said, a kitten might walk unhindered; and refused to believe in the greatness of Lamartine until she had determined that water could flow under his soles without wetting them. She said she disliked the British on account of their disgraceful pedal arches, adding that 'no great or noble achievement could be expected' from such a nation of flat-foots.

In 1838, and having spent money with extravagant abandon for more than a quarter of a century, she was left almost destitute when Lord Palmerston, the Foreign Secretary, impounded her pension as a sop to her creditors. Lady Hester bombarded Lord Palmerston and Queen Victoria with a series of insulting letters of complaint. When these elicited no response, she retreated into her palace and bricked up the gate. The following summer she died, aged sixty-three.

When rumours of her passing were communicated to the British Consul at Beirut, he at once set out for Dahar-Jûne to determine their truth. He found her sumptuous palace entirely bare, stripped to the walls by her Druce servants, most of whom had quietly slipped away into the hills. Only her personal attendants had remained behind. They had left their mistress exactly as they had found her. They stood too much in awe of her, even in death, to close her mouth or shut her eyes. Among her papers, the British Consul found a request that she be buried in her own garden, exactly on the stroke of midnight. In accordance with a second request, she was lit to her last resting-place by a single candle, fixed in the skull of one of her long-dead lovers.

If the image is a powerful one, it conjures up inappropriate associations. In old age, Stanley Baldwin became something of a dodderer and when someone remarked that he might almost be dead, Churchill countered: 'No, not dead. But the candle in that great turnip has gone out'. Like Gladstone, Baldwin suffered from a variety of nervous tics. He had a 'strange movement of the head, with half-closed eyes, like some tortoise half awake, smelling the air – blinking, snuffy neurotic'. His features were those of 'a disillusioned tram conductor' and he had the habit of 'smelling his notes and licking the edges slightly'. After the General Election of 1928 he ordered yellow curtains for his new home in Upper Brook Street, explaining that the light filtering through them produced the effect of brilliant sunshine. It may be that sunshine was singularly lacking in his life. F. E. Smith once remarked of Baldwin's policies: 'He takes a leap in the dark, looks round and takes another.'

A more cautious eccentric was Hannah Beswick of Cheetwood Hall in Lancashire who lived in fear of premature burial. At her death in 1758 she left £25,000 to her doctor, a man named White, on condition that he regularly inspect her corpse for signs of life for twelve months after her decease. Having a fear of draughty old vaults, White sensibly had her body embalmed and encased in a grandfather clock which he situated at the top of the stairs, the glass viewing panel masked by a tasteful tapestried curtain. He visited the body twice a year for the rest of his life, accompanied by a friend who acted as a witness. After his death, Hannah's remains found their way to the Manchester Museum of Natural History where they were displayed in a glass case. According to Timbs: 'De Quincey in one of his stories mentions it being taken from the case and the body of a notorious highwayman being substituted', but this seems to be no more than artistic licence. One hundred and ten years after she breathed her last, the trustees agreed that Hannah Beswick's death was beyond dispute and granted her a decent burial.

It was a callous age and not all ladies fared so well – as witness the case of the first Mrs Martin van Butchell. Her husband was a highly eccentric London dentist and egomaniac who blazoned his name above his door in twelve-inch-high marble letters and rode about the streets on a milk-white pony daubed with purple spots. At one time he sold 'cakes, gingerbread, apples, nuts and the like to children at his door' possibly to provide 'employment for his own children'. Each of his wives 'was told that the colour of her clothes must be limited either to white or black. The first chose black and the second white'.

Perhaps as a result of her husband's domineering ways, the first Mrs van Butchell left a will of calculated spite, ordering that her fortune pass to a distant relative 'the moment I am dead and buried'. Martin nullified this directive by not burying her at all. Instead, he called in the great Dr Hunter and had her corpse embalmed. Hunter fitted her out with a pair of glass eyes and filled her veins with oil of turpentine and camphorated spirit of wine. She was then dressed in her choicest (black) clothes, propped up in the drawing-room and put on public display from 9 a.m. to 1 p.m., Monday to Saturday.

The rush to view eventually forced van Butchell to restrict admission to people introduced to him through friends. When he remarried, his wife took a violent dislike to 'the dear departed' and ordered her out of the house. She was presented to Dr Hunter who added her to the exhibits in the Hunterian Museum, where she remained for more than a hundred and fifty years. When the museum was bombed, during the last war, she was destroyed down to the last fragment of her glass eyes.

Peculiarly enough, glass eyes have figured quite prominently in the history of eccentricity. Colonel Wintle possessed one; and Viscount Colville always kept a spare in a little gold ball suspended from his watch chain. In more recent times, John Christie, the founder of the Glyndebourne Festival Opera, loved to create a little amusement by using his as a prop. He removed it one night at dinner. After giving it a polish with his handkerchief, he popped it back, turned to the lady sitting next to him – who happened to be the Queen – and enquired: 'In straight, ma'am?'

Christie enjoyed muddling important people's names when introducing them; and for a period, presented all female visitors to the opera with knitting needles and wool. He owned one hundred and ten shirts and a hundred and thirty-two pairs of socks. As a result of having spent sixteen years as a master at Eton, he developed a passion for food of the school-dinner type and once consumed seven helpings of tapioca pudding at a sitting.

It has sometimes been alleged that Christie was not a true eccentric: that he lacked certain essential qualities – parsimony, suspiciousness and ill-temper. No such charge could be levelled against Father Denham who, until his death in 1953, was the vicar of Warleggan in Cornwall. He possessed all three traits in abundance. He detested his fellow men and so alienated his parishioners that they eventually ceased to attend his services altogether. This lack of a flock seems not to have worried him and he continued to preach each week to the cardboard effigies with which he replaced them. He surrounded his home with a high fence of barbed-wire and anyone wishing to see him had first to make an appointment. He awaited their arrival armed with a pocket watch, late-comers being turned away. The rectory was entirely devoid of furniture and its occupant existed on a diet of nettles and porridge. He did construct a playground for the village children in the garden; but it was never used, possibly because the adults could not forgive him for painting their church red and blue.

An equally depressing misanthrope was Lord Crewe, who was long remembered for two remarks which he made when his country-seat, Crewe Hall, was gutted by fire. At the height of the blaze he turned to his sister and said: 'On this occasion, at least, you cannot complain of your bedroom being cold'; and when the hoses of the firemen had reduced his mansion to a charred and blackened swampland, he said: 'I think I had better send to London for my galoshes'. He hated the sight of servants and any housemaid glimpsed about the corridors of Crewe Hall after ten o'clock in the morning was almost certain to be dismissed.

In this respect he had much in common with the irascible Lord William Russell who suspected that all servants were either slothful or downright dishonest. He considered having all the cutlery in the servant's hall engraved with his name and title, but prefixed with the words 'stolen from'. His overbearing ways eventually drove his valet, a man called Courvoisier, to murder him. One night, after the household had retired to bed, Courvoisier stripped naked, (presumably to avoid being splashed with his master's blood) padded along the corridor and cut Lord William's throat as he lay sleeping. He was hanged outside Newgate prison two months later. Forty thousand people turned out to witness this raree-show, among them Thackeray and Charles Dickens. The latter was so depressed by the experience that he was unable to work for two weeks.

The case had a strange sequel. Many years after, it transpired that the murder had been witnessed by the couple in a bedroom of a house nearby. As both the man and the woman were married to other people, they refused to testify to what they had seen for fear of the social consequences. Their dilemma was later used as the basis for a highly successful melodrama: 'The House Opposite'. Some decades after its initial success, the rights in this were offered to the eccentric theatrical impresario, Violette Melnotte, who shrewdly saw that as the sentiments were outmoded there could be no profit in it. Violette was a brilliant businesswoman with a deep attachment to money. But she cared nothing for her employees. When an actor attempted to kill himself by putting his head in the theatre oven, her only concern was to know whether she had the legal right to compel him to refund the price of the gas.

Chapter 7

The *Injured* Queen of England

Caroline of Brunswick-Wolfenbüttel, Consort Queen of George IV, stands at the centre of one of the most sordid tragedies ever to disgrace the British monarchy. Yet in reviewing it one is forced to much the same conclusion as the magistrate in 'The Lion and Albert': 'that no one was really to blame'. Given the preposterous character of the protagonists, things could hardly have ended otherwise. It is a classical example of the emotional conflict which results when two eccentrics meet head-on. The reverberations continued to affect Court life in England for the best part of a quarter of a century.

None of the Hanoverian kings were happy in their domestic relationships. George I had an unfaithful wife whom he imprisoned for the best part of thirty years and in consequence could hardly bring himself to look upon his son, the future George II. George II detested his own heir, Frederick, the much maligned Prince of Wales, and when 'Poor Fred' died – as the result of being hit by a tennis ball, which broke an abscess – he transferred his antipathy to his grandson, later George III, who looked with mortal terror on his grandfather all his life.

Not surprisingly as the Hanoverians gave so little affection, they generated none. The feelings of the common man were best summed up by Walter Savage Landor:

> George the First was always reckoned
> Vile, but viler George the Second;
> And what mortal ever heard

Any good of George the Third?
When from earth the Fourth descended
God be praised, the Georges ended!

George IV was probably the most comprehensively hated of all the Hanoverian kings. He was also a good hater. He abhorred his great-grandfather, loathed his grandfather and detested his wife. His dislike for his daughter, the Princess Charlotte, was so marked that when she died it was rumoured that he had procured her end by poison. Mackworth Praed wrote:

A noble nasty course he ran,
Superbly filthy and fastidious,
He was the world's first gentleman
And made that appelation hideous.

His course was so 'noble nasty' that before he was twenty years old his attempts to become the most fashionable man in Europe had caused him to fall victim to every Jewish money-lender in London. He was at his wit's end to know how to deal with the problem and frequently spoke of suicide. He endeavoured to mortgage his future by offering his creditors the astounding prospect of a double return on their money, together with an Irish peerage, if they would defer their demands until he became king. This offer was not accepted because nobody trusted him to keep his word. His finances were so straitened that when his carriage was held up in Hay Hill the highwayman's haul amounted in modern terms to less than fifteen pence.

As if this were not trouble enough, he formed an insane and unconstitutional attachment to a young widow named Maria Fitzherbert and resolved to marry her. Under the terms of the Royal Marriage Act of 1771 a union contracted by the heir to the throne without the prior knowledge and consent of the sovereign was automatically invalid. For this, and for other reasons, Maria refused him.

The Prince raged and wept, rolled on the ground, gnashed his teeth and paced about tearing his hair until the poor girl was driven to distraction and simply found it more expedient to give in. Nonetheless, as Maria was a devout Catholic and her husband the future head of the English church, the marriage had to be kept a closely guarded secret.

Had the Prince of Wales' love for his wife been fixed and steady, the country might have been plunged into a constitutional crisis which was in the event deferred until the tragically short-lived reign of Edward VIII. It was not. 'The First Gentleman of Europe' quickly tired of her. In a passionless sort of way he nonetheless continued to be fond of her and forty-five years later, as he lay dying at Windsor, his thoughts returned to her. Because he was wearing her miniature beneath his nightgown, he begged his attendants not to lay him out but to bury him in the clothes 'in which I shall breathe my last'.

Two years after his death, Maria approached the Duke of Wellington who a few days later called at her house in Tilney Street, Mayfair, to burn the collection of love letters which she had received from her royal husband. He had been a prolix correspondent and the task took two full days. Maria survived five years more and died in 1837, the year of Queen Victoria's accession.

Although she had been disgracefully ill-used, Mrs Fitzherbert bore her troubles with dignity and restraint. The same could not be said of her husband.

By the autumn of 1794, George's debts amounted to £375,000. Consequently, when his father George III decided that he should make a marriage, he was in no position to refuse. The King settled for this purpose on his niece, the Princess Caroline, the daughter of his sister, Augusta, and the Duke of Brunswick-Wolfenbüttel. The Prince was not consulted although it was tacitly understood that he would comply on condition that his father pay his debts. In this way – and almost by default – father and son sowed the seeds of a confrontation which was destined to rock the British monarchy to its foundations.

At the time the negotiations were set in train, Caroline was a mature young woman of twenty-six. Having passed the whole of her life at an obscure European court populated by frivolous, libidinous courtiers and popinjay groups dedicated to the pursuit of pleasure, the plotting of intrigue and backstairs amours, she had grown into a monumentally silly creature. She was distinguished by her loquaciousness, petty-mindedness and utter lack of discretion, qualities conspicuous in her mother. From her father she inherited a truculent, dogged courage. She never forgot it and later remarked: 'My father was a hero. They married me to a zero'.

Twelve years earlier, in 1781, John Stanley had visited the Court of Brunswick-Wolfenbüttel and encountered a very different young lady. He found the fourteen-year-old Caroline 'a beautiful girl . . . simply and modestly dressed . . . with light and powdered hair hanging in curls on her neck'. Her looks were animated and her lips those 'from which only sweet words would flow'.

We can only conjecture what occurred between Stanley's visit and the arrival, in 1794, of Lord Malmesbury to conduct by proxy her engagement to the heir to the British throne. Sir John's impressions may have been accurate at the time; but a few months after his departure an event occurred which radically altered Caroline's personality, her attitude to men and thereby the course of her life. That event was the marriage of her elder sister, the Princess Augusta, to the future King of Wurtenburg.

In 1781 the Princess Augusta took up residence at St Petersburg, the home of her husband. The couple were hopelessly incompatible and Augusta soon took a lover by whom she bore a child. When it became known that the child's father was a former admirer of the Russian Empress herself, the situation became impossible. Augusta was exiled to a castle in the Baltic.

News was eventually conveyed to Brunswick of Augusta's death 'of some putrid disorder, which made it necessary to bury the body immediately without waiting for any ceremonies due to the rank of the deceased'. The Duke, her father, was naturally suspicious but 'all further enquiries that were made ended in this account and no light was thrown upon the business'.

The circumstances surrounding her death have never been clarified. One source implies that she was put into the cellar of the castle where, because of the unusual atmosphere prevailing, her body remained in a perfect state of preservation until it was identified some years later 'and decently interred in the churchyard of Goldenbeck'.

An alternative theory suggests that tiring of her husband's incessant beatings, Augusta simulated death, was sealed in her coffin and subsequently escaped from Russia in disguise to join the father of her child. A Jewish mendicant appeared at the Court of Brunswick to swear on oath that he had seen her at the opera at Leghorn; and various accounts exist of her subsequent adventures in New Orleans and on the Island of Bourbon. None of them have been established beyond doubt.

The incident nonetheless had a profound affect on Caroline and from this date her character underwent a fundamental change. It was almost as though she had begun to think of the House of Brunswick as cursed. In that case, there was no hope for her. Fate would dispose of her as it chose: she would retaliate by throwing off all inhibition, by becoming herself.

Shortly after she came to this decision, her parents gave a Court ball. Caroline was thought too young to attend. She accepted the decision with apparent good humour; but at the height of the ball a servant suddenly appeared, in a state of great agitation, and summoned the Duke and Duchess to her apartment. The rest of the Court naturally followed. As the door was thrown open, Caroline was seen to be writhing semi-naked on the bed, her face like death. She moaned: 'I am in labour. Madame, I beg of you, find me an *accoucheur* at once!'

There were gasps and scandalised whispers, but when the doctor arrived Caroline ceased to scream. She rose from her bed and with great calmness crossed to the washstand and began removing the white enamel which she had used to give her face its deathly pallor. She turned to her mother and said in a cold voice: 'Perhaps, Madame, you will not keep me from a ball again'.

In his book *The Wanton Queen*, E. E. P. Tisdall remarks:

Some people have said that this incident proves that Caroline was mad from the beginning. It hardly does that. But it does show, however, that she had an erratic and perverted imagination, an unhealthy sense of humour; that she was a clever actress, cunning, a liar, amazingly self-possessed and a monument of determination.

The Court had hardly recovered its composure before this 'monument of determination' was again at the centre of a scandal. A voluptuous and libidinous girl, she was constantly exposed to men practised in the art of seduction. One day, she disappeared from Court and was heard of no more for several months. She eventually surfaced, as gay and empty-headed as ever – but there were those who hinted that she had 'known what it was to *love*'.

It was to this giddy young woman, in the autumn of 1794, that George III contracted his son. The precise arrangements were left to Lord Malmesbury, a trusted courtier of long standing. Privately, Lord Malmesbury had serious doubts as to the wisdom of the choice; as a dutiful servant of the Crown he could have none. On his arrival, he ran a jaundiced eye over the future Queen of England. He found that there was good and bad in equal measure. If she was short, she was nonetheless pretty with fine blue eyes set in a doll-like face. Her teeth were 'tolerable but going'. Her finest feature was her bust, which was full. 'The rest of her figure is not good.' Her manner he found 'open, frank and unreserved' – perhaps by English standards a little too unreserved. Her dress was slovenly and her toilette neglected. By discreet enquiry he learned that her undergarments were often disgracefully grubby. She had an antipathy to water and in typically forthright fashion remarked: 'They have only one bath at Versailles – and they grow flowers in that'.

On the afternoon of 3rd December, Caroline was summoned to her father and ordered to 'lie upon the couch'. Lord Malmesbury then entered the room and silently removed his right shoe and stocking. He then placed his bare leg on the upholstery beside her and Caroline became officially betrothed to the Prince of Wales.

In the time which elapsed before she could be conveyed to London, Lord Malmesbury endeavoured to impress upon Caroline the need for decorum in her new situation. She should not attempt to venture an opinion on any subject until she had been in England at least six months. It was all quite useless. One night, as his Lordship was relaxing before dinner, a page sidled up to him, clutching a handkerchief. He unfolded it to reveal a gory slime-covered tooth. He said: 'The Princess has commanded me to show you this, milord. She has just had it pulled and feels sure you will appreciate her high spirits'.

Because Malmesbury was fearful that the news would be secretly conveyed to the French, who might attempt to kidnap her, Caroline's departure was delayed for some time. A start was eventually made four days after Christmas. As a result of the general unrest then existing in Europe, it was three months before she set foot on English soil. In an over-excited state, she spent her one night at sea strolling about the deck in the company of one of the better-looking ship's officers, a Lieutenant Richard Boyle.

The vessel was met at Greenwich by Lady Jersey. As the Prince's acknowledged mistress, she was not the most appropriate ambassador and her selection may have been a calculated snub. Lady Jersey detested Caroline on sight and persuaded the rest of the royal family to detest her also. Queen Charlotte – who had rather thought to marry her son to a lady of her own choosing – joined with Lady Jersey in a vicious secret vendetta which made Caroline's life a misery for many years. Caroline lacked both the tact and the wit to turn their wrath. On the journey to town, and having known her companion for five minutes, she confided to Lady Jersey that she had left at Brunswick one 'whose little finger I love more than I shall ever be able to love the whole of the Prince of Wales'.

On hearing that his bride-to-be had arrived at St James' Palace, the Prince of Wales rushed over from his home at Carlton House to view her. When he entered the room where she was waiting, Caroline attempted to kneel. The Prince very gallantly drew her up and embraced her. Having done so he began to tremble, turned deathly pale and retreated to a far corner of the room. To Lord Malmesbury he called in a hoarse voice: 'Harris, I am not well. Pray, get me a glass of brandy'. Malmesbury asked whether His Royal Highness might not prefer a glass of water. 'No', said the Prince. After gulping the liquid down, he made an abrupt headlong departure, murmuring: 'I will go directly to the Queen'. The appalled Caroline turned to Lord Malmesbury and said: 'Mein Gott! Is he always like this?'

The dinner which followed was an even greater disaster. Caroline railled and bantered the guests in a very familiar manner, prattled on about people and events of which she knew nothing and made several coarse references to the Prince's relationship to Lady Jersey. After dinner, whilst they were waiting for the King and Queen to appear, the Prince remarked on the unsuitability of Caroline's shoes. She said: 'If you don't like them go and make me a better pair yourself'. Later in the evening she produced a bundle of letters for the royal family which she had brought over from the Court at Brunswick. 'Here you are' she said, tossing the bundle across the table in the direction of the King, 'these will prove to you that I am not an imposter'.

The marriage took place on the evening of Wednesday 8th April 1795 in the Chapel Royal of St James's Palace. The bridegroom came so epically drunk that he had to be supported to the altar by his two gentlemen ushers. He had consumed several glasses of brandy, a quantity of wine and acccording to the Duke of Gloucester 'went out after dinner and drank twelve glasses more of Maraschino'. At one point in the ceremony, overcome by the sight of his impossible bride – who was wearing too much make-up and a ludicrous beaver hat – he made a feeble attempt to rise from his knees, as though intent on flight. He was prevented by the King who left his seat and firmly pressed him down again.

The ceremony was conducted by Archbishop Moore. Being aware of the morganatic marriage to Maria Fitzherbert, when he reached that part of the service where it is customary to enquire after any impediment to a marriage, he fixed the Prince with a significant look. The Prince began to cry. The Archbishop transferred his stare to the King who, as he was probably the only member of the congregation not privy to the secret, could only look puzzled. It may be that he was remembering his own wedding in the Chapel, thirty-four years previously. His bride's heavy robes pulled down her dress with the consequence, said Horace Walpole, that 'the spectators knew as much of her upper half as the King himself'.

The wedding breakfast was nothing short of lunatic. The bridegroom became ever more drunk and kept turning towards Lady Jersey 'with a piteous and bewildered expression'. In her efforts to sprinkle a powerful emetic on Caroline's food, Lady Jersey hardly noticed.

The Prince spent just long enough in Caroline's bed that night to father the future Princess Charlotte. Having done so, he fell asleep in the grate. He never slept with his wife again. A less credible version suggests that, either as a result of his drunken condition, or some congenital defect, the Prince found it impossible to fulfill his marital obligations and that, 'Caroline having been rendered unconscious by means of a drug', another was introduced into the royal bedchamber in his place.

On the face of it, the idea seems preposterous. Yet it is not impossible that the Prince was impotent. With the exception of the Princess Charlotte, he had children neither by his two wives nor by his many mistresses; and his distaste for Caroline was transparent. To add to the mystery, the household was woken the following morning by the sound of screams and raised voices. The Prince was seen to exit from his wife's chamber in a dishevelled state, still dressed in the clothes of the night before. He stared about wild-eyed for a moment and then dashed away. We can only guess at what happened. Caroline's version of events clarifies nothing:

> Judge what it was to have a drunken husband on one's wedding day, and one who passed the greatest part of his bridal night in the fireplace – where he fell and where I left him! Time passed on and I was *enciente* – at least everybody said so but as for me, I pitied them because I was incredulous of my condition. Eventually Charlotte came into the world.

If the Princess Charlotte was not George's daughter then the uncanny resemblance which she bore to other members of the royal family would suggest that Caroline's lover that night was one of the Prince's brothers. The most likely candidate is the Duke of Gloucester, known as 'Silly Billy'. He displayed an almost dog-like devotion to Caroline and followed her everywhere.

The royal honeymoon was spent at Kempshott Manor where the company was largely made up of the Prince's blackguardly drinking cronies. With the significant exception of Lady Jersey, the Princess of Wales was the only lady present.

At dinner one evening, the Prince took the glass from which Lady Jersey was drinking and fixing his wife with a contemptuous stare, drank from it himself. Caroline turned to her near neighbour, Lord Coleraine, snatched the pipe from his mouth and puffed a great cloud of blue smoke into her husband's face. The company sat for several minutes in stunned silence.

In Europe such hoydenish behaviour might somehow be excused as the mark of gay good nature. In England, a country which outwardly pursued a rigid conventionality, it simply would not do. Her uninhibited manner affronted the Prince. He found it deeply repellent. It served to fix his dislike beyond all remedy and the couple were soon seeing as little of one another as protocol would permit. Nonetheless, when the Princess Charlotte was born, exactly nine months after the wedding night, the Prince suffered greatly. He claimed to feel every contraction intensely; and after the birth had to be carried to his bed in a swoon. For twenty-four hours there were genuine fears for his life. Being of sturdy German stock, Caroline made a somewhat quicker recovery.

If there were those who felt that the Prince's reaction augured well for an improvement in relations with his wife they were quickly disabused. Soon after the birth of the Princess Charlotte the couple's mental and emotional estrangement was given a physical embodiment when Caroline left London to take up residence at Shrewsbury House near Blackheath.

Although people were warned by the Prince that to visit his wife would render them *persona non grata* at Carlton House, Caroline remained airily indifferent. 'Oh, it is all in the common course' said she. 'People go to different inns: one goes to the King's Head, another to the Angel.' When this remark found its way back to the Prince it only served to increase his hatred. His wife was a source of embarrassment which he was powerless either to moderate or remove. Some years later, after he had become King, when an equerry announced the death of Napoleon with the words: 'Sire, your greatest enemy is dead', George started up, crying: 'By God, is she?'

Rather surprisingly, Caroline's staunchest ally during this period was the King himself. Perhaps because he felt guilty at having proposed the marriage in the first place, he regularly rode over to pay her a morning visit. For the rest of the time she occupied herself with local charities; pursued her interests in music and painting; became a more than passable sculptress; and fashioned exquisite little wooden toys which she daily presented to the local children who came to romp with her in her garden.

In the evenings she gave dinner parties. Initially, these were a great success. But her love of horse-play and the manner in which she openly leered at the young men ultimately frightened polite society away. Her character resembled that of Sir Kenelm Digby who 'would have made himself respected in any part of the world had he drop't out of the clouds . . . provided he did not stay there above six weeks'.

Caroline's pranks were often juvenile, but they were not devoid of purpose. When she wished her husband to believe that she had taken to drink, she had a large decanter of cold tea placed before her at dinner, representing it as brandy. She emptied it before the soup was cleared and by the following afternoon the story was all round Carlton House.

In 1801 George III appointed Caroline as Ranger of Greenwich Park. Much to the indignation of Queen Charlotte and the Prince of Wales, Caroline moved into Montagu House, the Ranger's official residence. It was a personal triumph for her, but not without its drawbacks. The Princess Charlotte was to maintain her own establishment at Blackheath under the management of a governess. Caroline objected. She was told that the King would consent to no other arrangement – although she might visit her daughter whenever she pleased.

There were soon reports of 'great goings-on' at Montagu House and the conduct of the Princess of Wales was described as 'lamentably unguarded'. On one occasion she told her lady-in-waiting, Lady Douglas, that:

> she got a bedfellow whenever she could and that nothing was more wholesome. She said that nothing was more convenient than her room; 'it stands at the head of the staircase which leads into the Park, and I have bolts on the inside, and have a bedfellow whenever I like. I wonder you can be satisfied only with Sir John!' She has said this more than once. She has told me that Sir Sidney Smith had lain with her; and that she believed all men like bedfellows, but that Sir Sidney better than anybody else; that the Prince was the most complaisant man in the world; that she did what she liked; went where she liked, and had what bedfellow she liked, and the Prince paid for all.

Caroline eventually confided in her lady-in-waiting once too often. Lady Douglas was then heavily pregnant. One day she called for a saline draught to ease a bout of nausea. Caroline called for another and downed it at a gulp. Lady Douglas was astonished. What could have possessed her to do such a thing? She could hardly stand in need of it. Caroline replied: 'Yes, I do. What do you look at me for with your wicked eyes. You are always finding me out!' She added that there was no cause for alarm. Her husband should not get to hear of it. As she already received numerous small children at Montagu House – helped with their maintenance and assisted with their education – one more would hardly be noticed.

The Douglases saw little of the Princess of Wales during the latter months of 1801. When they returned, at the end of January 1802, Lady Douglas was shown into the drawing room of Montagu House where she saw a child lying on the sofa, covered with a piece of red cloth. As she later deposed: 'The Princess took me by the hand, led me to the sofa, and said: 'There is the child. I had him only two days after I saw you'.

At this point, Caroline seems to have come to her senses. Terrified by the thought of what might result if her confidences became common knowledge, she decided to sever acquaintance with the Douglases at once. She did so in a totally inept way. She wrote to Lord and Lady Douglas saying that she could no longer receive them. Lady Douglas wrote back asking to know the reason. Her letter was returned unopened.

A few days later, Sir John Douglas received a scandalous but anonymous letter which alleged that his wife was having a passionate affair with their mutual friend, Sir Sidney Smith, who lived with them. The sentiments were couched in the coarsest possible terms and 'the missive was decorated at the top by crude drawings of an obscene nature, apparently meant to show the guilty pair making love'. Although it had come in the normal manner, by the twopenny post, it bore the imprint of a seal which both Sir John and Lady Douglas had frequently seen on the desk of the Princess of Wales.

Two days later Caroline wrote to Sir John and Lady Douglas enclosing what purported to be a second anonymous letter repeating the allegations. The Princess claimed that as this had been addressed to her she had been fully within her rights to open and read it. Because of its scandalous content, she could no longer receive either the Douglases or Sir Sidney.

Lady Douglas was so deeply upset by the affair that the Duke of Kent was driven to intercede on her behalf. Lady Douglas declined his help 'out of consideration for Her Royal Highness's rank'.

There the matter might have come to a rest. But after a year, word trickled through to Carlton House that the Princess of Wales had given birth to an illegitimate son – a boy she was now endeavouring to pass off as 'William Austin', the son of an out-of-work dockyard hand from Deptford.

It is doubtful whether the Prince of Wales believed the story. But it offered two heaven-sent opportunities to be revenged on his wife. If the allegations were true, she was morally depraved and as such might safely be denied access to the Princess Charlotte. If it could also be established that she intended to represent the boy Austin as the legitimate product of her marriage – an act which might ultimately lead to young William inheriting the throne of England – there might also be grounds for a charge of High Treason. This was indeed a heady prospect.

It was decided to establish 'A Delicate Investigation' into the true parenthood of the boy. The proceedings were held in camera and were hopelessly unconstitutional. The Princess was granted neither legal representation nor the right to attend. If she was found guilty, she stood to lose her head, but her fate was to be decided not by a judge, sitting in open court and buttressed by the weight and panoply of the law, but by a panel of lay commissioners. Their verdict was to be communicated directly – and only – to the King.

In the event, Caroline retained her head. The commissioners severely reprimanded her for her general conduct, but concluded that there was 'no foundation for believing that the child now with the Princess of Wales is the child of Her Royal Highness'.

It was almost certainly the right conclusion – although, given young William's appalling disposition, he undoubtedly merited Caroline as a mother. A spoilt, slovenly ill-mannered creature he developed into a coarse and stupid young man who died, still young, in an Italian lunatic asylum.

In a tardy attempt at democracy, a copy of the commissioners' report was forwarded to the Princess of Wales at Montagu House. She promptly wrote to her father-in-law requesting that now her name had been cleared he receive her once more at Court. She hinted that in the event of his non-compliance she would hand the commissioners' findings to the broadsheet-sellers. Good-humoured as ever, he not only agreed, but – to the great mortification of the Prince and his party – granted her apartments in Kensington Palace.

For the next two years Caroline lived a life of relative quietude. Her greatest sadness during this period was the death of her father, mortally wounded at the battle of Jena by a hail of shot which struck him in the face. He was led from the field hiding what was left of his features behind a gory handkerchief, his troops cringing away in horror.

In 1811, George III's mind became permanently unhinged and the Prince of Wales was appointed to rule in his stead. Two years later he decreed that his wife was no longer morally fit to associate with their daughter. Caroline retaliated – as she had threatened to do in the matter of the 'Delicate Investigation' – by carrying the issue to the press. As her husband was universally detested, she quickly became a national heroine. The Regent counter-attacked by ordering an enquiry into her household expenses, a petty-minded piece of harrassment which rebounded on him. The investigating parliamentary committee concluded that the Princess had been disgracefully short-changed over the years and voted her an allowance of fifty thousand pounds per annum.

Displaying an uncharacteristic flair for public relations, Caroline wrote to the press, thanking parliament for its generosity, but pointing out that as she was acutely aware of the 'burthens' under which the British people were currently labouring her conscience would not permit her to accept more than was 'sufficient to my expenses', a mere £35,000. This resulted in a further increase in her popularity. The Regent was seen as a vicious degenerate implacably opposed to anyone and everyone who had the temerity to set themselves against him.

Unlike Sir Kenelm Digby, Caroline did not outstay her welcome. Having attained the zenith of her popularity – and being at last provided by parliament with sufficient funds – she determined to quit England and set out on her travels.

In October 1814 she chartered a vessel to take her first to Germany, then to Italy. The night before she was due to sail, the captain stumbled out of a dockside tavern in an alcoholic haze. He was promptly slapped on the back by one of the royal Princes who said: 'You're going to take the Princess of Wales in your ship. Well, sir, you'll be a damned fool if you don't make love to her'. Caroline never tired of recounting this story.

Through the good offices of the Governor of Lombardy, she acquired a seedy Apollo named Bartomoleo Pergami to act as her courier. A penniless Italian peasant, he became the instrument through which she learned to enjoy her new-found freedom. He had a fondness for Ruritanian-style uniforms, a gargantuan appetite – and considerable personal charm.

Another lady of rank floating rather aimlessly around Europe at this time was the Empress Marie Louise, the wife of Napoleon Bonaparte who was then languishing on Elba. Having struck up an acquaintance, these two outrageous women caused a considerable stir at Berne where, 'in very bad taste', they sang saucy duets in the local taverns and made naughty jokes about their abandoned husbands.

Continuing on her giddy way, Caroline next materialised at Lausanne where she gate-crashed a fashionable *masque*. Having exhausted all her partners, she danced on alone until dawn, whirling and dipping like some frenzied gypsy girl. At Rome she was received in audience by Pope Pius VII. The same evening, and having left off her corsets, she attended a ball wearing a dress which began below her waist. The upper half of her body was covered only by a piece of loosely draped gauze.

Although she was not at first aware of it, her antics were being closely observed and catalogued. Her husband's spies followed her day and night, reporting her every movement to London. The Prince had no doubt that when he eventually succeeded to the throne, Caroline would attempt to return to England and claim her rights as Queen. When that day came, he intended to be forearmed. It did not go unnoticed that Pergami was soon promoted from courier to equerry; or that he breakfasted with Her Royal Highness every morning. It was also a matter of common knowledge that Caroline left her bed each night 'in a little white nightdress and carrying her pillow under her arm' and did not reappear until well past dawn. When the party was at sea, Pergami and the Princess slept on deck in a tent.

Having reached the Holy Land, Caroline made a twelve-mile pilgrimage on foot to Bethlehem, founding the Order of Caroline of Jerusalem to which she appointed Pergami Grand Master. She also made friends with a contortionist dancer, Mahomet the Turk, who was later called as a witness at Caroline's trial and required to recreate his obscene dances for the benefit of the House of Lords.

On a visit to Baden, Caroline shocked the local community by riding about with a pumpkin on her head – which she said helped to keep her cool – and in the spring of 1817 turned up in Milan. Here she attempted to organise a carnival. When the Governor learned that she intended to ride at the head of the carriage procession distributing not sugar-plums but large quantities of coin, he forbade it, fearing a riot.

In December 1817 this giddy round of pleasure was temporarily halted by the death of the Princess Charlotte. A stolid, stupid but essentially pleasant young woman, Charlotte's short life had been far from happy. Prior to her marriage she had lived at Warwick House where, according to Wheatley, 'the entrance . . . was secured by bars of iron on the inside'. As a result, she could only gain access to her apartments by going through the adjoining residence of Carlton House, the home of her father. In May 1816 she married Prince Leopold of Saxe-Coburg after jilting the Prince of Orange, the husband selected for her by the Regent. She died giving birth to a still-born son in November 1817. In her last moments, she called out to her one true friend, Baron Stockmar, 'Stocky, they have made me drunk'. Gronow relates that 'the *accoucheur* who attended her was so much affected' by this that 'he committed suicide . . .' Fourteen years later, her husband was elected King of the Belgians.

On receiving news of her daughter's passing, Caroline fainted and remained in a paralytic trance for twelve hours. She quickly recovered, however, and was soon railling against the tiresome tradition of mourning. 'I do so hate black – it is so unbecoming.'

At the beginning of 1820 George III died and the Prince Regent ascended to the throne of England as George IV. As he knew she would, his wife at once arranged to return to England. Accompanied by her ill-assorted retinue, she landed from the Calais packet at midday on 5th June 1820. The last thunderous movement in what has been called 'the great British symphony of madness' was about to begin.

Hysterical with joy at the prospect of the inevitable confrontation with the King, Caroline's raggle-taggle supporters descended on London, sweeping their champion across Westminster Bridge to cries of 'God Save the Queen' and 'Down with the King'. Forty thousand artisans presented her with a Loyal Address. The Mayor of Hammersmith proffered a Declaration of Sympathy.

A month to the day from her landing, the King struck back. In an attempt to deprive her of her title he introduced a Bill of Pains and Penalties into Parliament, charging the Queen with adultery and High Treason. It was an unprecedented step and for some time the country teetered on the brink of civil war. Several regiments – notably the Third Guards and the Tenth Hussars – were deeply sympathetic to the Queen's cause and a hurricane of protest swept through the country during which the King was burned in effigy.

On the morning of 17th August – and wearing an enormous black hat topped with ostrich feathers – Caroline drove to the House of Lords to stand her trial. As her accusers arrived they were jeered, pelted with rotten fruit and required to shout 'God Save the Queen' under pain of injury. Even the great Duke of Wellington was not exempt. He gave in with a good grace. 'Since you will have it so,' said he, 'God Save the Queen – and may all your wives be like her.'

According to Creevey, Queen Caroline dismounted from her carriage and with the cries of her supporters still ringing in her ears, 'popped all at once into the House, made a *duck* at the throne, another to the peers, and a concluding jump into the chair which had been placed for her'.

The capital charge of adultery was considered first. The peers, fearing the ugly mood of the country, and the likely consequences if they were to find her guilty, ruled that if she *had* committed the offence it was probably with a foreigner, in the course of her travels, and therefore of no consequence. Caroline, as sly as ever, said that she had only once broken the seventh commandment 'and that with Mrs Fitzherbert's husband'.

The peers next turned their attention to an examination of the Queen's general behaviour in the hope of discovering grounds for depriving her of her title. The King's spies had done their work and the prosecution was able to muster a host of foreign chambermaids, tavern-keepers and washerwomen to depose at length on her indiscretions.

Charged with the Queen's defence, Lord Brougham saw that there was to be no effective rebuttal. But he was quick to spot the weakness in the prosecution's case. In order to make its point, it had relied almost entirely on the Queen's foreign servants. Brougham countered by calling only English witnesses of unimpeachable reputation and rank. It was a blatant appeal to the court's inherent snobbishness – and it worked.

Brougham's closing speech runs in typescript to three hundred thousand words, the equivalent of five modern novels. It represents one of the finest and most eloquent pleadings ever heard at the English Bar. As a result, the Bill of Pains and Penalties was passed, at its third reading, by a mere nine votes. This meant that Caroline had been found guilty in theory; but in practice would suffer no consequences.

The subtlety of this was lost on the common people who saw in it the utter vindication of their champion. When the result was announced they swept into Old Palace Yard and cheered Caroline to the echo. But the trial had solved nothing. The country remained cursed with a King and Queen who heartily detested one another, could not live together, and were fundamentally opposed on every point of mutual interest.

Flushed with success and now more determined than ever to assert her rights, Caroline wrote to her husband demanding that the coronation fixed for 19th July should be a joint one. She was cooly informed that this was out of the question. If she were foolish enough to present herself at the Abbey she would find the doors barred against her. She wrote again, enquiring what manner of dress it would most please the King to have her adopt for the Abbey. She was told: 'a winding-sheet.'

Nothing could have been more calculated to harden her resolve. On the morning of the great day she left her rented house in South Audley Street determined to be crowned Queen of England. As she had been warned would be the case, she found the doors of the Abbey guarded by six pugilists, among them Tom Cribbe and 'Gentleman' James Jackson. When an usher approached and asked for her ticket, she said: 'I am the Queen'. The usher replied that he had strict instructions to admit no one except by ticket; 'Not even though she is the Queen'.

If she had hoped to be swept through the doors of the Abbey on the shoulders of the masses she was doomed to disappointment. The mob had tired of her. None of the soldiers saluted. Nobody in the crowd called upon God to save her. She was reduced to running from entrance to entrance, shrilly demanding admittance. When she realised that she had been out-manoeuvred she retired defeated. Lord Penryhn watched her drive away. As an old man, he remembered that: 'the expression on her countenance was the most diabolical thing I ever looked upon in my life'.

Even now she refused entirely to give up. She wrote to the King demanding that he arrange a separate coronation for her within the week. Her letter went unanswered.

Her spirit was broken. Eighteen days later, as she lay abed at Brandenburgh House, she told the man who had so ably defended her before the House of Lords; 'Brougham, I am going to die, but it does not signify'. Brougham said that her physicians were confident she would make a full recovery. Caroline said: 'Well, I know better than them. I tell you I shall die, but I don't much mind it'. At ten-thirty that evening, just as a gust of wind blew in at the window of her room, making the curtains sway and dance as once Caroline herself had danced – at Rome, at Parma and at Carlsruhe – she died at the early age of fifty-two.

She left instructions that the plate on her coffin should be inscribed: 'Caroline: The *Injured* Queen of England'. It was not allowed. Her body was conveyed home to Brunswick and quietly interred in the family vault. By a strange coincidence, the captain of the vessel entrusted with the task of taking it on the first stage of its journey across the Channel was none other than Richard Boyle who, twenty-six years earlier, as a young Lieutenant, had kept Caroline company in her nocturnal pacings about the deck of the ship carrying her to England for her wedding.

George IV survived his wife by ten years, dying in 1830. In the last days of his life his physicians became afraid to inform him of his true condition and when the end came he clutched the hand of his page and whispered: 'Wally, what is this? It is death, my boy. They have deceived me'.

When his wardrobe was emptied, the pockets of his various coats were found to contain a hoard of banknotes with a face value of more than £10,000. A statue was erected to his memory in Trafalgar Square. It is a poor thing. The matching plinth, which stands parallel to it, is vacant and likely to remain so – there has never been a pendant to George IV.

Chapter 8

The Family Sassoon

The Sassoons have sometimes been called 'the Rothschilds of the East'. They were. But they were also much more. Displaying a facility for adjustment which was nothing short of astounding, they transformed themselves from relatively humble beginnings as tax-collectors in Baghdad into the greatest mercantile dynasty the orient has ever known. Having done so, they moved to England where they adapted with such success to an environment completely alien to their traditions that they ended by weaving themselves into the very fabric of London society – becoming almost more English than the English.

The founder of the modern dynasty was David Sassoon, born in 1792. Descended from a long line of Jewish courtiers and merchant princes who claimed to be able to trace their descent from King David, he grew up in Baghdad, once a rich and prosperous trading capital but now a city in decline.

By the time he had grown to manhood, Baghdad was ruled by the cruel and uncompromising Daud Pasha, who instituted a vicious campaign of extortion against several of the minority groups which populated the city. As a rich and prominent figure in the Jewish community, David Sassoon became a particular target. In 1829 he was arrested, threatened with death and only released on payment of an enormous ransom.

Reasoning that Daud Pasha would continue to persecute him, bleed him dry and kill him anyway, David sewed some pearls into the lining of his jacket, equipped himself with a money belt and escaped by sea the evening he was released, disguised as a rabbi. He settled firstly at Bushire, a dingy Persian fishing port, where he spent his first night in a quayside warehouse beleaguered by a horde of enormous rats. He kept them at bay by shooting the more aggressive ones with his pistol.

He made a new if modest start as a peddler, but for some reason business failed to prosper. One day he encountered a fortune-teller who told him that all his efforts would be doomed to failure until he went to India. David accepted this advice and moved to Bombay where he opened a small counting-house, supplementing the turnover by importing raw opium.

In 1835, three years after the move to India, David's second wife, Farha Hyeem, gave birth to a son which they named Reuben. He was to grow up into a jaunty, flashy, deeply complex man. He could solve the most intricate financial problems with a few deft calculations on his starched shirt cuff; yet he would never permit his mattress to be turned on a Friday. It was Reuben who eventually pioneered the route to London.

Reuben was speedily joined in London by one of his younger brothers, Abraham, who quickly adopted western ideas and dress and took to calling himself Arthur. A third brother, Abdullah, joined them soon after, changing his name to Albert in honour of the British Queen's husband. He never really thought of himself as anything but English and was so intensely patriotic that when the Prince Consort died he paid three thousand pounds to have a statue erected to his memory.

In 1864 old David Sassoon died, 'a quill pen still in his hand'. His estate was valued at more than five million pounds. Thanks to the trade in cotton and raw opium, his interests in merchant banking and excursions into property development, the Sassoons had grown very rich indeed; but the magnificence and ostentation of their life-style in the orient could never be adequately reproduced in England. When Reuben's sister, the crippled Mozelle, visited him in London she was astounded to discover that he occupied only one mansion in Lancaster Gate and not the whole crescent. She would have been even more astonished by the topsy-turvy house he was later to occupy in Belgrave Square. For some reason the stables were situated on the roof and every time Reuben wished to drive out he had to order his horses and carriage to be sent down in a lift.

Within fourteen years of their arrival in England, the Sassoons had begun to insinuate themselves into society. Their heady, almost indecent advance was naturally resented and stories of Sassoon brashness and pretension were legion. When a visitor to the Alfred Sassoons declined a slice of lemon in his tea and asked for milk, the butler is alleged to have replied: 'Jersey, Hereford or Shorthorn?' Aline Sassoon was singled out for particular odium and held up to ridicule as the very worst sort of parvenu. It was said, quite without foundation, that she had asked an acquaintance to recommend 'some deserving old aristocrat as I have a vacancy for a hall-porter'.

Family dignity suffered a further blow at the hands of old Mrs S. D. Sassoon. Noticing the Brighton police were feeling the heat, she sent them a consignment of melons. Her husband eventually dropped dead – in public – in the lobby of the Langham Hotel. The reserved English dismissed this as just another example of oriental flamboyance.

Matters were not improved when Rachel Sassoon married Frederick Beer. Not long after Frederick began to exhibit signs of *folie de grandeur* by clipping out the family crest on the back of his poodle, Rachel acquired *The Observer* and *The Sunday Times*, using the leader columns to promote such improbable causes as cannibalism. She had a total disregard for money, quite unacceptable to the English, and frequently hired trains at £25 a time in order to visit friends in the

London suburbs. Rather predictably, she eventually suffered a nervous breakdown. When Frederick died, she at first refused to have him buried and held long conversations with his portrait. She lived the last twenty-five years of her life in an enormous mansion, formerly the property of Judge Jefferys, cared for by two devoted nurses. From 1903 her affairs were administered by the Lunacy Commissioners. At her death in 1927 the Commissioners put her newspapers up for sale at a joint asking-price of £5000. They had been so devalued that the offer had to be withdrawn through lack of interest.

Perhaps the most exotic of all the Sassoons was Edward and Aline's son, Philip. He developed at Eton a passion for collecting pen-nibs; and at Oxford he became so unpopular that he was driven round Tom Quad at the point of Julian Grenfell's stock-whip.

On his father's death, Philip inherited a London mansion – most recently the site of the Playboy Club – and several country houses. Being something of an exquisite, he contrived like Beau Brummel before him at a mannered effect by magnifying the trivial and minimising the significant. In fact, he worked extremely hard at being effortless. When someone complimented him on his garden, he said: 'At twelve noon on the first of August each year I give a nod to the head gardener who rings his bell and all the flowers pop up'. The truth was even more bizarre. He spent a small fortune each year, selecting a series of coloured cigarette cases with which to demonstrate to that bell-ringing gardener the exact gradations of yellows and greens and blues he wished reproduced in the flower-beds.

A natural courtier, he served throughout the Great War as private secretary to General Haig and at the cessation of hostilities accepted a similar post with Lloyd George. A talent for brilliant gossip and habitual flattery made him something of a celebrity-hunter. One Easter a malicious acquaintance sent him a telegram which read: 'Christ is risen. Why not ask Him to lunch?'

Philip came to hero-worship Lloyd George and whenever he stayed at Park Lane or Port Lympne made a point of feeding him the 'virility breakfasts' of offal, kidney and liver which the little Welshman craved. One morning he shocked the prime minister by producing his late mother's pearls from beneath his shirt. He said: 'I carry them around with me to keep them alive'.

His predilection for feeding 'square meals into celebrated round holes' engendered in certain quarters a strong dislike and it was for some time rumoured, quite wrongly, that Evelyn Waugh had used him for the model of Anthony Blanche in 'Brideshead Revisited'. The rumour was lent credibility by his elegant manner, dandified dress, precocious aestheticism and odd lisp. Sir Harold Nicolson thought him 'the most unreal creature I have known' and 'un-English', which of course he was. At Cherkeley one evening, Max Beaverbrook was playing cards with members of his house-party when someone asked where Philip might be. Max said: 'Oh, I expect he is off flattering someone'. At this point Philip glided from behind a pillar and said: 'But not you, Max, not you'.

For all these feline witticisms, there was no harm in him. 'His baroque was worse than his bite.' When a waiter he knew confessed that he was in danger of losing a prospective job for lack of a dress suit, Philip donated one of his own. On learning that one of his most virulent critics was too poor to educate his son, Philip provided the wherewithal anonymously.

In an attempt to give the lie to rumours of Sassoon brashness he cultivated an air of modesty which occasionally rendered him more humble than Heap. One day, returning to his home in Park Lane, where a collection of paintings was being exhibited, he joined the queue and paid five shillings at the turnstile rather than give the impression of rudeness by pushing to the front.

He had an intense dislike of the sea – which he thought might claim him given the chance – and one evening the mischievous F. E. Smith had the engines of his yacht started up simply to frighten him. He had a strong premonition of his early demise, which is said to have been hastened by a bout of immoderate laughter brought on by learning that the family black sheep had been offered a virgin for £25. He had always loved flying and on his death in 1939 left instructions that his ashes were to be scattered over the gardens of one of his country mansions from an aeroplane. This went off without incident – although ash-scattering is not in the general way an exercise to be undertaken by the inexperienced. George Bernard Shaw – who believed that 'earth burial should be made a criminal offence' – had his own ashes hand-mixed with those of his wife on the kitchen table at Ayot St Lawrence. Within days of being deposited in a flower bed they had turned into a solid pancake which proved so durable that guides took to including it in their tours. When Emerald Cunard requested that her ashes be scattered over Grosvenor Square, the scene of her social triumphs, the task was entrusted to the art dealer, Sir Robert Abdie. He chose to execute the commission on a windy day. As he said later; 'I think the Square got rather less of Emerald than I did'. Another person who attempted the task, under similar circumstances, was 'combing her mother out of her hair for weeks'. After years of drudgery producing fifth-rate scripts as Metro-Goldwyn-Meyer, the writer Bud Schulberg left instructions that his ashes be blown in the face of Louis B. Meyer.

Philip's enthusiasm for air-flight was shared among the fourth generation of Sassoons by his cousin, Victor, who in 1909 became a founder member of the Royal Aero Club. Three years later he acted as co-pilot in the Grand Prix to Hamel.

At the outbreak of the Great War, Victor enlisted for flying duties with the Royal Naval Volunteer Reserve as an Observer. He was then thirty-three. On a gusty bleak morning in February 1915 he and his pilot took off on a reconnaissance mission over France. They had not been up many minutes when a spring broke in one of the engine's automatic inlet valves. Victor's legs were coated in burning oil. The pilot succeeded in bringing the plane down but Victor shattered his thigh and broke both legs. He remained a cripple for the rest of his life, unable to walk anything but short distances.

Unlike Philip, Victor could never bring himself to play the courtier. Nor was he prepared to waste his money – although he could, under certain circumstances, be extremely generous. One day a friend called at his office and requested a loan. Victor was late for an appointment. As he flew from the office, he called over his shoulder: 'As a banker I am unable to do it. I'll make you a gift of it instead'. He was as good as his word and the man duly received the money in the form of traveller's cheques. He also received an account for the stamp duty endorsed 'with the compliments of Sir Victor Sassoon'.

On another occasion, an impoverished but distant relative approached Victor for a loan. As he appeared too coy to specify the amount, Victor passed his cheque book across the desk and instructed him to fill it in himself. He rightly reasoned this would turn out to be less than the sum required – thereby leaving the door open for a further request at a later date. The second request was abruptly refused.

Sir Victor had a great interest in horseracing and confided to an acquaintance: 'There is only one race greater than the Jews and that is the Derby'. He found the competitive nature of the sport extremely stimulating, although he was always careful to maintain an air of nonchalance in victory. In 1925 he invested more than one hundred thousand pounds in building his own private racecourse at Poona; and eventually established a stud at Newmarket, although he knew that he would have to win a minimum of £100,000 each year in prize money to maintain it.

He spent more than half a million pounds in seeking to fulfil his dream of breeding a Derby winner, finally succeeding in 1953 with Pinza. After the race the Queen was heard to sigh and say to Sir Victor: 'Why ever did Pinza have to come on in the same year as Aureole?' According to Stanley Jackson: 'Pinza knew his manners'. When the Queen visited his stable he shook his mane and all but curtseyed.

In the late 1950s Sir Victor's health, which had never fully recovered from the flying accident of 1915, began seriously to deteriorate and a pretty, vivacious Texan nurse named Evelyn Barnes was hired to look after him. Unlike his other servants, 'Barnsie' refused to be intimidated by her autocratic employer and despite a forty-year age gap they developed a very companionable relationship. This mellowed into love and at the age of seventy-seven Sir Victor married her. Asked why he had not married before, he said: 'It takes a lifetime to acquire the judgement to *choose* the right wife'.

Two years later, after refusing to cancel a dinner on the grounds that he would not deprive his guests 'of their curry just because I am not quite up to the mark', he became ill and had to be confined to an oxygen tent. It soon became apparent that he was dying. Just before he did so and in a last assertion of his dislike of waste, he turned to Lady Sassoon, who was preparing an injection for him, and said: 'I'm not going to need that one, Barnsie'.

He was survived by his second cousin, Siegfried, the war poet, perhaps the most famous of all the Sassoons. At the time of Victor's death, Siegfried was seventy-five, having been born in 1886 to Alfred Sassoon and Theresa Thorneycroft – who had married Alfred on the rebound after being callously jilted by a farmer in preference for a barmaid. Although Siegfried was to recall his childhood with almost rapturous delight in *The Weald of Youth*, his parents were an ill-assorted couple and their marriage was not happy. Alfred eventually tired both of his uneventful life and Theresa and ran away to Kensington with her best friend.

Perhaps because his mother was careful to nurture his budding talent, Siegfried's formative years were spent in a world of daydreams and books. 'I had mermaids on the brain.' At Malvern he won a half-crown prize in a poetry competition organised by one of the masters; but despite his obvious talents left Cambridge without obtaining his degree.

In 1914 he was commissioned in the First Battallion, Royal Welch Fusiliers and posted to France. His initial attitude was one common to his class. (Twenty years later it manifested again among the young men who volunteered for the International Brigade.) War was a jolly jape: an opportunity for the happy-go-lucky idealist to display daring and courage in dangerous but highly stimulating – and therefore not quite real – situations.

Prior to the battle of the Somme and armed only with a handful of grenades, Siegfried attacked a German outpost single-handed. The Germans decamped. On reaching their position, Siegfried sat down and read his book.

It was the reality of war, the carnage and callous waste of human life, which ultimately outraged his idealism. It found expression in his poetry which became increasingly ferocious and abrasive. It was not only a protest at war – but at this war and those who were in charge of it. His attitude was best summed up by his poem, *The General*:

> 'Good morning; good morning!' the General said
> When we met him last week on the way to the line.
> Now the soldiers he smiled at are most of 'em dead,
> And we're cursing his staff for incompetent swine.
> 'He's a cheery old card,' grunted Harry to Jack
> As they slogged up to Arras with rifle and pack.
>
> But he did for them both with his plan of attack.

Just as the French generals were 'entirely let off' after the shattering defeat of Blenheim, so two hundred years later their British counterparts were forgiven their victory. In 1919 Field-Marshal Haig was offered an earldom. He at first refused it on the grounds that his means were insufficient to maintain the dignity. Parliament voted him a supporting grant of £100,000.

On the Hindenburg Line, Siegfried had his closest shave of the war. Leading his platoon in a charge aimed at reinforcing the Cameronians, he encountered heavy losses and was forced to retreat. He again left the safety of the allied trenches and with just six men attacked an enemy position. His lance-corporal lost his life and Siegfried was wounded in the neck. He nevertheless continued to advance – on his stomach – and throw his grenades. The platoon felt certain he would receive the Victoria Cross. His superiors recommended the Distinguished Service Order. As the engagement ultimately proved inconclusive, he got neither.

When he recovered from his wounds he was posted firstly to Palestine and then to France once more. Within a short time of his arrival he embarked on a one-man sortie to make a sketch of the enemy's position. He was severely rebuked for this by the brigade commander, but when he found that his drawing was lacking in certain detail went out once more to finish the job. As he was returning, a sniper's bullet hit him on the head. The force of the blow was assimilated by his tin hat. But it was nonetheless an incapacitating injury and he took no further part in the war.

In middle life Siegfried came to recognise what he termed as 'the tragic hopelessness of the class struggle' and joined the Labour Party. He also became a Roman Catholic. He continued until his death in 1967 to dress in a manner popular at Cambridge sixty years previously; and this, together with his rather awkward bearing, sometimes aroused suspicion. When he paid a visit to one of the Sassoon properties, the gardener eyed him with distaste and sharply told him to: 'Take yourself off'. Siegfried was greatly amused by this and later wrote several poems under the pseudonym 'Tak Yussof Hoff'.

He continued to play an excellent game of cricket and remained until well past seventy an especially gifted batsman 'not easy to dislodge except by bumpers'. He lived to be eighty and in the last years of his life Oxford University made him an honorary Doctor of Literature.

As he sat in the Sheldonian, decked out in that 'preposterous wig and gown, listening to the speeches' and gazing at the painted ceiling, one wonders whether there drifted into his mind some distant echo of old Baghdad – or of old David Sassoon squatting on his haunches in a quayside warehouse, on his first night in Persia, shooting rats with his pistol.

Chapter 9

Contrasting Oddities

There is a Shavian maxim which suggests that all progress depends upon the unreasonable man. If this is so, then the eccentric is surely the greatest benefactor known to history. The odder the theory, it seems, the more likely it is to be endorsed. Lord Monboddo was convinced that all babies were born with tails and persuaded others to believe this also. He refused to abandon the idea even after witnessing the birth of his own children, preferring to think that the midwife was part of a world-wide conspiracy to cut off all children's tails at birth.

Another specious theorist was Glenn Wilbur Voliva who believed the earth was flat. He began life as a disciple of John Alexander Dowie, a religious fanatic who emigrated to America in 1888.

Dowie was a plausible charlatan who attracted a considerable following as a faith healer. With the money he made he purchased ten square miles of land north of Chicago and built a township on the shores of Lake Michigan, populating it with his disciples and christening it Zion City. Within its precincts his rule was absolute. He disliked sex, oysters and life assurance, fulminating against all three from the pulpit of his church. So that the community might be self-supporting, he built a number of factories to manufacture lace, confectionery and furniture.

Had he not been an evangelist, Dowie might have ruled over Zion City for many years. But it was not sufficient to have converted its inhabitants; the rest of the world had to be convinced of his odd theories also.

He mounted a costly propaganda campaign which brought him to the brink of ruin. In an attempt to salvage something from this, he called in his old friend and former disciple, Glenn Wilbur Voliva. As Voliva was then living in Australia, it was some time before he could answer the summons. When he arrived he found Dowie had suffered a crippling stroke and was now a mere shadow of his former self.

Having made a fortune of ten million dollars from the manufacture of chocolate-covered biscuits, Voliva reasoned that Zion City could only be saved if he took over the role of Chief Administrator himself. When he came to examine the accounts of Dowie's Apostolic church, he discovered a discrepancy of two million dollars. He accused his old friend of polygamy and a disgraceful love of luxury. In 1905 Dowie was banished from the community. The disgrace was too much for him and he died, insane, two years later.

Voliva now set about imposing his own rule upon Zion City – a rule even more bizarre than his predecessor's. Lipstick, scanty clothes, high heels and swimming costumes were all forbidden, together with cigarettes and alcohol. No butcher, chemist or doctor was allowed to practice within the precincts of the city; nor were there any theatres or cinemas. All the sixteen thousand inhabitants were required to be off the streets not later each evening than ten o'clock. Anyone offending against these edicts was liable to arrest by Voliva's 'Praetorian Guard', an eccentric unofficial police force whose members were distinguished by arm patches depicting in silhouette the Dove of Peace. Their helmets were inscribed with the word 'Patience' and they wore at their belts not clubs but miniature bibles. As no one in Zion City was permitted to whistle, sing or drive a vehicle in excess of five miles per hour, arrests were frequent. Offenders were either summarily fined or carried before Voliva and required to listen to a one-hour lecture on their sins.

From time to time the law-giver also gave lectures in support of his flat-earth theories. He was convinced that the world was saucer-shaped, that the north pole stood at its centre and that the south pole was represented by a sort of crustated boundary of ice which ran the length of the perimeter. The heavens were no more than a super-structured dome from which the sun, the stars and the moon were suspended like celestial chandeliers. After ruling over Zion City with despotic sternness for twenty years, Voliva was ruined by the depression. By the time he died, in October 1942, his religious theories and principles had been discredited.

An equally bizarre theorist was the European reformer Francesca Nortyuega who believed that even the most insignificant of God's creatures have souls. As a result, she left a vast fortune to her niece on the understanding that she equip the only other beneficiary, her pet goldfish, with a pair of pants. The idea would have amused Thomas Birch, a Keeper of Books at the British Museum in the reign of Queen Victoria and a fanatical angler. He used to stand at the river bank disguised as a tree, his arms represented as branches, his fishing-line as blossom. He believed that any movements he made would thus be mistaken by the fish 'for the natural effect of a mild breeze'.

A third nineteenth-century eccentric who cultivated the art of astonishment for astonishment's sake was George Francis Train. A penniless orphan, he was packed off to his maternal grandmother at the age of six with a label pinned to his coat. The sea journey to Massachusetts took twenty-three days and Train wore the same suit of clothes throughout. On his arrival he was set to work on the family farm. He next became a grocery store assistant, drudging for up to eighteen hours each day in return for fifty dollars a year. He was rescued from this by a distant but wealthy relative who found him a position in his shipping business. Within two years he had been promoted to manager. He increased profits by building larger and faster ships and by indulging in a little opium smuggling.

By the time he was twenty-one, Train had become rich and successful; but when he selected as a bride a young woman whom his patron thought unsuitable, the partnership was dissolved. Train and his wife set sail for Australia where, thanks to his drive and charismatic personality, he became as influential as he had formerly been in America. When twenty thousand workers in the Ballarat and Bendigo minefields rebelled against increased licence fees imposed by the government, and decided to set up their own Democratic Five Star Republic, they offered Train the presidency. He very sensibly declined; but when the rebellion crumbled, he found its leader a job as a stevedore aboard one of his boats, smuggling him out of the country quite literally under the nose of the Chief of Police.

Given his restlessness and love of adventure, it was always likely that Train would become a dedicated traveller. In 1870 he journeyed around the world in eighty days, thus providing Jules Verne with the inspiration for his popular novel. The exploit made Train famous overnight – but he would never agree to meet Verne, believing the writer owed him a debt which had never been full acknowledged. 'Jules Verne', he said, 'translated my fact into fiction.'

The feat spawned a host of imitators. One of these was a reporter from *The New York World*, a rather intense and hysterical young woman named Nellie Bly, who broke Train's record by eight days. The day she completed her marathon, her newspaper recorded the feat in a banner headline: 'Father Time Out Done!' Nellie became a source of endless public interest and remained so until her death in 1922. During this period songs were dedicated to her and babies and racehorses named in her honour. There were even Nellie Bly games.

Train announced plans for an even speedier circumference. This was thought to be so foolhardy that he was brought before a Boston judge and declared insane. He was taken to the Tombs prison and placed on Murderer's Row. Here he met William J. Sharkey, another unusual individual. As the prison system was then heavily corrupt, Sharkey eventually escaped by dressing as a woman and walking to freedom with the aid of a stolen visitor's pass. He fled to Cuba where he lived out the rest of his days.

Train, meanwhile, had become something of an embarrassment to the government and the prison governor was instructed to allow him to escape by leaving open the door to his cell. With splendid effrontery, Train declined the offer, insisting on a fair trial. In the end a compromise was reached. A panel of doctors was appointed to examine him. They found him to be 'of unsound mind but harmless'. He was released soon after.

Capitalising on the incident, Train now took to calling himself 'The Great American Crank' and announced his intention of running in the forthcoming presidential election as Dictator of the United States. His campaign was disadvantaged by his refusal to shake hands with potential supporters – but he made amends by shaking hands with himself. When the results were announced it was revealed that he had received not a single Electoral vote.

Train was able to indulge in these attention-grabbing escapades as a result of his association with the Atlantic and Great Western Railroad. The construction had been a huge undertaking, involving the laying of four hundred miles of track across three states. Although he was directly involved in none of the work, he received more than one hundred thousand dollars for negotiating the initial contracts.

He was also responsible for introducing the tramcar to London. The first two miles of track were laid between Bayswater and Hyde Park, on an experimental basis. The project was not a success. The residents took exception to the noise and the bustle and, when a child was knocked down and killed, Train was arrested and accused of manslaughter. The charge was eventually dropped.

In the last years of his life, George Francis Train became a sad figure. His incessant lust for attention caused him to dream up ever more outrageous stunts, many of which landed him in prison. People were at first amused by these, urging him to even greater follies. But when he emerged from his cell for the fifteenth time he discovered that the great American public had grown bored with his antics.

As his derangement increased, so his wealth evaporated. Success had come too easily and when fortune ceased to smile upon him he found himself increasingly unable to cope. Destitute and alone, the man who had once boasted personal expenses in excess of two thousand dollars per week, passed his declining years in a flea-pit hotel. On the night of 19th January 1904 he died of Bright's disease at the age of seventy-five. For two days he lay in state in a New York funeral parlour while two hundred people filed past his bier. A post-mortem examination of his brain established that, measured against those of the great, it ranked twenty-sixth.

If Train failed in his efforts to persuade the American people to allow him to govern them, he was by no means the only eccentric to make the attempt during those years. A second candidate, and one who fared rather better, was the Englishman, Joshua Norton. Like Train, Norton was a rich man who grew increasingly odd after falling on hard times.

Born in London in 1819, he emigrated firstly to South Africa, then to Brazil. At the height of the Californian Gold rush he moved to San Fransisco where, resisting the siren call of the panhandler, he shrewdly opened a general store. As a result, and within the space of six years, he accumulated a fortune of a quarter of a million dollars. Flushed by success, he next endeavoured to corner the market in rice – and was ruined.

The setback unhinged his mind and in 1857, claiming that the government was corrupt, he announced that he would for the future rule America in person as Emperor Norton I. Having annexed the title of 'Protector of Mexico', he proceeded to hold court in his room in a seedy lodging-house, administering his empire by studying bus timetables and inspecting local sewers. In a remarkably short space of time he became an accepted 'character'. He was admitted to theatres free of charge and audiences rose on his entrance.

He was held in great affection and when an over-zealous policeman was foolish enough to arrest him on a charge of vagrancy, public outrage forced City Hall not only to drop the charges but to issue an official apology. The Emperor accepted this with characteristic graciousness and urbanity. The City of San Francisco endeavoured to make matters up to him by granting him free board and lodging for life.

For all this, Joshua never relaxed in the presence of officialdom; and when the Central Pacific Railroad refused him a free meal aboard one of its trains, he retaliated by 'abolishing' it. Lesser mortals profited from Central Pacific's mistake; and when the Emperor levied a small weekly tax on shopkeepers in the Bay area, most of them paid up with wry good humour rather than risk incurring his displeasure.

With the passage of the years, Norton succeeded in routing the soulless bureaucrats who had plagued him for so long; and when he announced that his 'Imperial Wardrobe' had grown disgracefully shabby, City Hall rushed to replace it. In 1880, and at the relatively early age of sixty-one, he died. He retained the loyalty and affection of his subjects to the end and more than three thousand people attended his lying-in-state.

Another king-struck individual who attained some prominence during this period was James Harden-Hickey, who developed delusions of grandeur after meeting Napoleon III. On a journey to India he 'discovered' the Island of Jamaica and finding it unpopulated, proclaimed himself king.

On returning to America he set about turning his dream into reality. He issued a glossy prospectus, together with a series of stamps, and undertook a fund-raising campaign, hinting at the existence of a fabulous buried treasure. In order to provide 'an instant proletariat' for his kingdom, he arranged for five hundred Chinese coolies to be shipped to the island.

Shortly before he was due to sail, his dreams were shattered by news that the British had 'invaded' Jamaica with the intention of setting up an engineering project. Harden-Hickey protested, but in the end was forced to admit defeat. Ironically, as soon as he did so (but for reasons of their own) the British abandoned the island. By way of consolation, Ralston J. Markowe offered him the 'kingdom' of Hawaii. Harden-Hickey petulantly declined it, preferring to spend his last years nursing his grievance and attempting to interest other wild-eyed adventurers in a plan to invade England.

To raise money for this, he travelled to El Paso where he vainly attempted to sell his one remaining asset, a farm. Stranded and without funds, he wired his family for help. When none came, the man who had once written a best-selling treatise on suicide took poison. The trunk under his bed was found to contain just three items: the 'crown' of Jamaica; the faded letter offering him the throne of Hawaii; and a copy of his book on suicide. When the news of his death was conveyed to his wife, she said that she was 'sorry to hear of it', but refused to accept delivery of his corpse.

It seems to be the fate of a certain type of American eccentric to be not much mourned. When 'the Greatest Man in the East', Timothy Dexter, arranged a mock funeral for himself the results were so far from being what he had expected that he was forced to cane his wife in the kitchen for not crying enough.

Dexter was a merchant prince who, like many a blockhead before him, endeavoured to buy his way into society but failed because 'he would neither be hypocritical nor keep his mouth shut'. He later wrote a book entitled 'A Pickle For The Knowing Ones'. As it was entirely devoid of punctuation, he became known as 'The Foe of Grammar'. One wit said it was a work which would be read 'when Shakespeare and Milton are forgot, but not *until*'.

Dexter adorned the garden of his house at Newburyport, Massachusetts, with a series of columns fifteen feet high, surmounting them with colossal images of 'statesmen, philosophers, Indian Chiefs and allegorical figures representing Fame and Liberty'. When one or other of these fell from favour they were changed by 'a few brushes of the paint into someone else.' They continued to stand until toppled down by 'the great tornado gale of 1815.' After Dexter's passing they were sold at auction, none realising more than five dollars.

In order that the world might share in his treasures, Dexter opened his garden to the public. Unfortunately, he had a tendency to 'take improper liberties with the fairer sex' and the number of visitors soon diminished. Ladies continued to come. But they were 'the less scrupulous of their sex' and there were instances 'of his getting most sadly used by such guests . . . for sometimes a half a dozen country damsels made him a visit for a frolick and protected each other.' They also went 'laden from his gates with fruit and flowers'. Thwarted in his purpose, 'the Greatest Man in the East' raged about the house and cursed his family.

He may have had good reason to do so: they were all imbecile. Mrs Dexter was a slattern, her son a dunce and her daughter a 'giggling belle'. According to Samuel Knapp: 'the fame of her father's wealth brought about her a host of swindling, simpering *gallantes*; but most of them retired after a visit or two, finding it impossible, for all their love of money, to bring their minds to make serious proposals to one so entirely unfitted for society'. She eventually married 'a grave philosophical scholar', but after the birth of her only child, her mind became unhinged and she was supported for the rest of her life 'by the provident care of her father'.

Dexter's son, Samuel, believed that his father's wealth 'could supply the place of everything'. As a boy he was 'capricious in his appetite, petulent [sic] in his temper and cowardly in the extreme'. At school he 'bribed his fellow pupils with cakes and fruit and confectionery, to assist him in getting his lessons. The only ingenuity and talent he ever exhibited was in inventing lies to screen himself from punishment. The boys despised, and the masters pitied, his imbecility'.

After leaving school, this Bunteresque creature began to think himself a grand fellow and importuned 'his father to send him to Europe in command of a vessel'. Mistaking a costly education for a good one, Timothy agreed, although not without certain misgivings. The boy squandered the cargo in gambling, 'at which he was a mere gull'.

Dexter had an altogether better head for business. On one occasion a malicious clerk employed by a rival merchant persuaded 'the

Greatest Man in the East' not only to purchase an enormous quantity of warming pans but to ship them, ludicrously enough, to the West Indies. Dexter turned the tables by removing the covers from the pans and having handles attached to them. He represented these as 'skimmers' and the pans as 'ladles'. He sold both to a large sugar refiner who was so pleased with them that he ordered more, calling them 'the best machines of their kind ever invented'.

When Dexter's wife left him, he and his worthless son turned the Newburyport mansion into 'a squalid bagnio'. The beautiful curtains, formerly the property of a Queen of France, became 'stained, unseemly and offensive'. The books in the library were the envy of many a gentleman, but Dexter 'never read in them ten minutes at a time'. According to Knapp: 'the libidinous prints were often much worn, and many books were entirely despoiled . . . The library when sold amounted to a trifle only'.

In his efforts to ape the Boston upper classes, Dexter next purchased a team of cream-coloured mares which exactly complimented the colour of his carriage. These were for a time greatly admired, but when his enthusiasm – 'unstable as the wind' – began to wane, 'he sold them for no other fault than they would not change colour as his fancy changed'.

When an acquaintance informed him that no gentleman's establishment could be considered complete unless it possessed a collection of paintings, Dexter employed a discerning and knowledgeable young man to scour Europe on his behalf. This connoisseur returned with an excellent selection, but 'Dexter chose all the daubs and declined taking the others'. When he realised his mistake, 'he had them marked with the signatures of Correggio and Guido, Raphael and Titian' and passed them off as originals.

Timothy Dexter was rich: yet through the paucity of his soul, he ended in destroying the beauty of his elegant mansion – despoiling the priceless furnishings and decorating the walls with worthless pictures. He might better have followed the example of the artist Capitsoldi who was very poor and lived for some years in an attic in Warwick Street, Soho. 'Being without furniture', Capitsoldi proceeded 'to paint chairs, pictures and window curtains on the walls of his sitting-room; and so admirably were these executed that, with an actual table and a couple of real chairs, he was able to entertain on occasion a friend in an apartment that appeared more or less adequately furnished.'

With the exception of Capitsoldi – and perhaps Jack Gainsborough – the world of art has produced few genuine eccentrics. William Blake is almost – but not quite – disqualified by his hallucinosis. He is too much of a divine child. His startling trick of walking to the horizon and touching the sky with his finger – of holding conversations with Julius Caesar and trees filled with angels – renders him more nearly mad than eccentric. His wife, Catherine Boutcher, on the other hand, does qualify – if only because of her matter-of-fact

acceptance of her husband's singularity. Towards the end of his life, when he spent much of his time closeted in his room, deep in conversation with the Archangel Gabriel, Mrs Blake was heard to remark rather plaintively: 'I see so little of Mr Blake nowadays. He is always in Paradise'.

In contrast, Jack Gainsborough was a genuine artist-eccentric, but he was never as successful a painter as his brother Thomas, and ultimately turned his talents to inventing. He produced a cuckoo which sang all year round and a haystack that walked. He possessed a remarkable imagination which, coupled with a painstaking ingenuity, produced results as startling as they were useless. As a boy he coated every apple on a tree in a local orchard with dough. He then cooked each apple individually by standing on a ladder and allowing it to rest in a saucepan heated by means of a chafing dish held beneath it. When the task was completed, he fetched a neighbour, an old soldier by the name of Addison, to admire his handiwork. Colonel Addison asked what it was meant to represent. Gainsborough said: 'An Apple Dumpling Tree'.

A more serious boyhood jape was perpetrated by Thomas de Quincey, the author of *Confessions of an Opium Eater*, who in 1802 turned up in London almost penniless after running away from Manchester Grammar School. He approached a lawyer and money-lender named Brunell. Having satisfied himself by discreet enquiry that he could in time expect to be repaid, Brunell advanced the seventeen-year-old boy a small sum of money and provided him with lodgings in a derelict house which he owned in Soho. Thomas repaired to Greek Street and found:

> On taking possession of my new quarters, that the house already contained one single inmate – a poor friendless child, apparently ten years old; but she seemed hunger bitten . . . From this forlorn child I learned that she had slept and lived there alone for some time before I came, and great joy the creature expressed when she found that I was in future to be her companion through the hours of darkness.

That night the ill-assorted pair:

> lay upon the floor, with a bundle of law-papers for a pillow, but with no other covering but a large horseman's cloak. Afterwards they discovered in a garret an old sofa cover, a small piece of rug, and some fragments of other articles which added a little to their comfort.

De Quincey and his pathetic little friend lived from hand to mouth, eating scraps. These were occasionally supplemented with bits of food which de Quincey acquired on his nocturnal walks. He refused to go abroad during the day as he 'dreaded beyond all other evils the chance of being reclaimed by his guardians'. During one of these moonlight strolls he encountered a sixteen-year-old street-walker named Anne. She befriended him 'and for many weeks he walked at night up and down Oxford Street or rested with her on steps or under the shelter of porticos'. His presence can hardly have increased Anne's trade; but then Anne was an uncommonly tender-hearted young woman.

> One night, when we were pacing slowly along Oxford Street, and after a day when I felt unusually ill and faint, I requested her to turn off with me into Soho Square. Thither we went and we sat down on the steps of a house . . . Suddenly as we sat I grew much worse. I had been leaning my head against her bosom, and all at once I sank from her arms, and fell backwards on the steps. From the sensations I then had I felt an inner conviction of the liveliest kind that, without some powerful and reviving stimulus, I should have died on the spot, or should at least have sunk to a point of exhaustion from which all re-ascent, under my friendless circumstances, would soon have become hopeless. Then it was, at this crisis in my fate, that my poor orphan companion, who had herself met with little but injuries in this world, stretched out a saving hand to me. Uttering a cry of terror, but without a moment's delay, she ran off into Oxford Street and in less time than can be imagined, returned to me with a glass of port wine and spices, that acted upon my empty stomach (which at that time would have rejected all solid food) with an instantaneous power of restoration; and for this glass the generous girl, without a murmur, paid out of her own humble purse when . . . she had the bare necessities of life and when she could have no reason to expect that I should ever be able to reimburse her.

A short time after this incident, de Quincey was located by his guardians and through a stupid but characteristic piece of carelessness lost contact with Anne. He was beside himself with grief and to the end of his days was never able to pass the spot at which she had saved his life without being overwhelmed anew by worry as to what had become of her.

After his marriage in 1816, de Quincey earned a modest living by contributing articles to the numerous literary magazines which then flourished in London. He had his greatest success with a piece called *Murder Considered as One of the Fine Arts*, originally published in Blackwood's Magazine. The inverted logic, the droll humour, the finely woven ideas and the simple uncluttered prose, for once untainted by his fatal attachment to digression, make it one of the most amusing essays ever written on the subject. 'If once a man indulges himself in murder,' says the author 'very soon he comes to think little of robbing; and from robbing he comes next to drinking and sabbath-breaking and from that to incivility and procrastination.'

Although he did at some periods manage to reduce his intake of opium from as many as eight thousand to eight hundred drops a day, de Quincey never overcame the drug. It robbed him of his teeth and reduced his skin to the semblance of cracked parchment. He floated through his days in a waking dream. He was utterly incapable of dealing with the practicalities of life and when his lodgings became impossibly cluttered with books, he merely closed the door, turned the key and moved elsewhere.

The loss of his wife and two sons within the space of three years caused a deterioration in his mental condition. Thanks to the influence of Coleridge, he was now drinking five or six wine glasses of laudanum a night and his absent-mindedness also increased. Poring over his manuscripts by candle-light he frequently set light to his hair. He seldom noticed this himself and if told about it simply tousled his locks with his hand and carried on working. When his manuscripts caught fire, however, his response was nothing short of galvanic. Because the ink would have run, he refused to allow them to be doused with water and insisted on smothering the fire with cushions. He was hopelessly unco-ordinated and the exercise nearly cost him his life.

In practical affairs de Quincey was helpless to the point of imbecility. He was incapable of dressing himself unaided, would muddle the simplest errand and was so naive with money that for long periods his address had to be kept secret in order to afford some remission from the eternal baying of his creditors.

On one occasion he approached a friend for a loan of seven and sixpence (thirty seven and a half pence) proffering by way of security a screwed-up piece of paper which he referred to as 'a document'. When this had been unravelled, it proved to be a fifty-pound banknote.

Despite these minor aberrations, his extraordinary gifts never quite deserted him and he took an almost childlike pleasure in demonstrating them. In this he was reminiscent of the violinist, Niccolò Paganini, who was so vain that he purposely played on frayed strings in the hope that one of them would break – thus giving him the opportunity to display his virtuosity on those remaining.

If one trait characterises eccentricity as much as any other it is a certain type of hyperactivity. Its practitioners become madcap dynamos, invested with an almost inexhaustible lust for life. They pursue experience with an intensity of purpose which burns them out before their time. As they tend to have a similar effect on others, we will expose ourselves here only to three: Jack Mytton, Charlotte Cibber and Jemmy Hirst.

Jack Mytton, Squire of Halston in Shropshire, was a 'fast-living gent' who hunted naked, setting his horse at impossible fences and throwing bundles of bank-notes to the populace as he passed. A confirmed scapegrace, he drove his gig into rabbit warrens at high speed – in order to see whether it would overturn – ran races with the clouds and once jumped a toll-gate in a phaeton. Having bet a friend that he and his horse Baronet could outrun him home, he gave the man a fifteen-minute start and won by a cool three minutes by taking a short-cut through a deep lake. He never learned to swim and had Baronet unseated him he would almost certainly have drowned.

He was a reckless gambler who seems not to have cared whether he won or lost. One night, returning in his coach from a race meeting at Doncaster, he fell asleep whilst counting the profits. It was a gusty evening and when he awoke he found his winnings had blown out of the window. No escapade was too outrageous for the 'eccentric, open-hearted, open-handed Squire of Halston' and he astonished guests at a dinner party by making his entrance riding astride a bear. He regularly drank in an evening eight bottles of port – and as many of brandy. In the space of fifteen years he dissipated a legacy of three hundred and fifty thousand pounds and mortgaged beyond repair an income of ten thousand pounds. As a result of this wayward extravagance, he was committed as a debtor to the King's Bench prison where in 1834, at the age of thirty-eight and having set fire to his nightshirt in the hope of curing the hiccups, he died. His last words were: 'Well, the hiccups is gone, by God'.

The youngest daughter of Colley Cibber, the renowned eighteenth-century actor, Charlotte Cibber was a rebellious hoydenish child who took very young to the stage where she developed a mania for playing male roles. She starved with strollers, failed as a grocer, and was made bankrupt as a puppet-show proprietor. She married and was soon after widowed. Having remarried and been widowed for a second time, she was thrown into prison for debt. On her release she took to dressing as a man and caused a beautiful young heiress to fall in love with her. In order to escape the lady's unwelcome advances, she obtained a position as valet to an Irish Lord. Following this, she became by turns a sausage maker, waiter and tavern keeper. After being again made bankrupt, she wrote her autobiography in a shack, 'a pair of bellows on her lap by way of a desk'. It was not successful. She persevered and produced a novel with 'a cat, a dog, a magpie and monkey' for company. This also failed. In a fit of despair she dressed as a highwayman and attempted to rob her famous father in his coach. She died on 6th April 1760.

The career of Jemmy Hirst is distinguished from that of Charlotte Cibber in one important respect: Jemmy had money. In consequence he possessed a freedom to indulge his whims which Charlotte never knew. He filled his best coffin with punch in order to drink the health of his guests – and converted his second-best coffin into a prison with automatic doors. People unwittingly trapped within were forced to place a coin in an internal slot to escape.

Jemmy's reputation eventually reached the ears of Charles II and he was invited to court. Here he plundered the King's cellars, wearing a hat which measured nine feet in circumference; taught a pig to jump hurdles; rode a bull named 'Jupiter' in preference to a horse; produced homemade bank-notes with a face value of fivepence halfpenny; and had sails fitted to his carriage and was soon after blown as a result 'into a draper's window'. He died, aged ninety, having left instructions that his body should be carried to the grave by twelve elderly virgins. He would have been the first to appreciate the joke when only two could be found.

Eccentrics such as Hirst, Mytton and Charlotte Cibber are life enhancers. Arraigned against them is a breed of life-denying human brute epitomised by John Camden Neild.

Neild inherited in youth a fortune of £250,000 and became 'a

confirmed miser dedicated to the heaping up of riches'. In order to increase his wealth he married the daughter of John Camden, a descendant of the great antiquary and kin to the earls of that name. One of Mrs Neild's nearest relatives was another human brute. Edmund Pratt, a 'remarkable example of unconquerable taciturnity'. He seldom spoke and never whilst playing cards. On a voyage to the East, the vessel in which he was travelling was buffeted in a terrible storm off the Cape of Good Hope. Shipwreck appeared inevitable. When the mast-top lookout shouted 'Land Ho!' there was general rejoicing. Grown men hugged one another with joy. According to the *Eccentric Mirror*: 'at this the features of Mr Pratt were observed somewhat to alter and unbend. "I knew", said he, "you would enjoy the sight of land; I saw it an hour before the careless ragamuffin aloft." And these were the first, the last and the only words he uttered during the journey.'

John Camden Neild possessed considerable property at North Marston in Buckinghamshire; and when he was forced to undertake the repair of the church roof, he replaced the solid old wooden covering with strips of painted calico and supervised the work by sitting all day on a ledge of the steeple where he consumed his lunch of hard-boiled eggs, dry bread and buttermilk. He trusted nobody and daily counted the trees on his estate in case one should have been spirited away overnight. Rather than pay for a seat in a coach he accepted a lift on a coal cart.

This 'frigid, spiritless specimen of humanity' ultimately rendered his life so unremittingly bleak that he tried to kill himself. He was saved at the eleventh hour by one of his tenant's wives. On his death in 1852 he left his fortune of a million pounds to Queen Victoria for her personal use. The lady who had saved his life, and the housekeeper who had served him faithfully for twenty-six years, received not one penny. Deeply embarrassed by this, Her Majesty made provision for them herself.

Female misers are relatively uncommon. One of the least known is the American millionairess, Hetty Green. Although she was thought to be worth in excess of eighty million dollars, she existed in a fireless tenement on a diet of onions and eggs, laundering only that part of her petticoats which showed. When these wore out she replaced them with newspapers.

The obsession with not lighting fires is widespread among eccentrics of a certain type. When a sitter to the sculptor Joseph Nollekens was sufficiently incautious to remark on the lack of heat in the artist's studio, the miser of Dean Street struck him out of his will.

A third fire-hater was Daniel Dancer, a Harrow farmer who, when a friend presented him with a dish of trout, found himself faced with a hideous dilemma. He could not eat it cold for fear of the toothache. To eat it hot would have entailed lighting a fire. He warmed the dish through by sitting on it.

Born in 1716, Dancer is said to have displayed 'one of the most remarkable instances of the insatiable thirst for gold in the history of human nature'. His only food was a 'sticking' of beef, which was boiled each Sunday together with fourteen hard dumplings. This had to last the week. During one of his walks on the common, he found a sheep which had apparently died of disease. In order to supplement his diet he dragged it home and had it made into mutton pies, which he pronounced delicious.

When his sister lay dying, he refused to call a physician, saying: 'If her time has come [medicine] cannot help her and she may as well die now as at any future period'. He fed her on dumplings and sticking of beef and said that 'if she did not like it she might go without'.

Miss Dancer possessed a small property which she had proposed to leave jointly to her friends, Lady Tempest and Colonel Holmes, but died before she could sign her will. Her brother impounded her estate in lieu of 'thirty years board at £30 per annum'. In the last two years of her life he calculated her maintainance at £50 per annum because 'she had done nothing but eat and lie in bed'.

Dancer never took snuff but was quick to solicit a pinch from those who did, surreptitiously dropping it into his own snuff box. When this was full, he took it to a chandler's and exchanged it for a farthing candle 'which was made to last until he had again filled his box'.

On his death, in October 1794, at the age of seventy-eight, Dancer's hovel was found to be a veritable treasure house. Two thousand five hundred pounds were found in a dung heap in the cowhouse and two hundred pounds in the chimney. Attached to the teapot was a note which said: 'Not to be hastily overlooked'. Inside was six hundred pounds. He left most of his fortune to Lady Tempest, who had nursed him in his last illness. Unfortunately, the experience had so weakened her that she followed him to the grave three months later.

Dancer is said to have known 'all the *miserables* in the metropolis' and was a particular friend of the Southwark stockbroker-miser Jemmy Taylor, with whom, one evening, he contracted to dine. Shortly before the appointed hour, two banker's clerks looked in and found Jemmy boiling a solitary mutton chop 'in an *ocean* of water'. When he left the room, the clerks picked up three half-penny candles lying on the table and pitched them into the pot. When Jemmy next met them he accused them of stealing his candles. They told him what they had done and said that 'unless he had eaten them he would find the wicks at the bottom of the pot'.

In 1793, as Taylor lay dying, he sent for the parish officers of St Saviours and presented them with twelve hundred pounds on condition that they pray for his soul for a fixed number of years. As a stockbroker, he was used to receiving a discount for prompt payment and insisted that in consideration of such a large sum they increase the term by ten percent.

A second Southwark miser and one who, like Daniel Dancer, used his body to heat his food was John Overs, the local ferryman. He kept a large black pudding beneath his shirt which he warmed by the action of his rowing. Although black pudding then cost something like a penny a yard, Overs deeply resented having to share it with his servants. As he grudgingly doled out their allowance he would say: 'There you hungry dogs. You will undo me with eating'. In order to save himself the expense of feeding them for a day, he feigned death, reasoning that respect for his memory would prevent them from eating until they had seen him decently interred. Unfortunately, he had kept them so short that the moment he was laid out on a trestle and covered with a sheet, 'they began to dance and skip around the corpse'. They ransacked the kitchen, broke open the cupboards, and fetched out the bread, the cheese and the beer. This was too much for Overs to bear. Unable to contain his fury he 'stalked forth in his sheet . . . a candle in each hand'. One of his apprentices, thinking he was seeing a ghost – or a devil – caught hold of a broken oar and struck him dead.*

As soon as he heard of Overs' death, his son-in-law posted away to London to be with his wife. Unfortunately, he rode so fast that as he careened through the city gate his horse threw him, killing him instantly. His wife had thus to bury both her husband and her father. Being an upright, humane sort of man, the former was given a proper funeral. John Overs, because of 'his usury, extortion and sordid way of life', had been excommunicated and it was at first impossible to obtain any kind of Christian burial for him. The friars at Bermondsey were eventually prevailed upon to lay him to rest in their Abbey. This they did without informing the Abbot, who was then out of London on business. When he returned he had the body exhumed and placed on an ass. The ass was then turned out of the Abbey gates 'to wander where it would'. It ambled away towards St Thomas-a-watering, then a place of public execution, where it shook Overs off 'under the gallows'. Remembering his grudging character and avaricious ways, a group of local people dug a grave and unceremoniously bundled him in. Her spirit broken by her dual loss, his daughter entered a nunnery, using her father's fortune to found the church of St Mary, London Bridge, later renamed St Mary Overs in honour of its benefactor.

As with Howard Hughes, the true miser-eccentric is distinguished by a reluctance to part with things. Whether the object is of value or not is inconsequential. Possession is all. The results are sometimes

*He was acquitted of his master's murder on the grounds that Overs had lost his life 'through his own contrivance'.

amusing, sometimes not. When Catherine the Great of Russia discovered that she was suffering from dandruff she imprisoned her hairdresser in an iron cage for three years rather than have the news bruted about the court; yet she could be surprisingly sentimental. One morning, many years after her death, Count Bismarck arrived at court for an audience with the Czar. Having been shown into an ante-room overlooking an enclosed courtyard he noticed a lone sentry pacing the lawn below. When he was summoned to the Czar, Bismarck enquired after the man's function: there appeared to be nothing to guard. The Czar was as puzzled as his guest, but consented to look into the matter.

It transpired that many decades previously Catherine had woken one morning and, looking from her window, spied the season's first primrose. In order that no one should pick it, she had posted a sentry to guard it. The sentry and his descendants continued to patrol the lawn long after the primrose had gone simply because no one had thought to countermand the order.

A similar story is sometimes told of Queen Victoria at Balmoral. One morning, soon after her accession in 1952, the present Queen is said to have looked into a backstairs cupboard – and discovered a bottle of whisky. That evening it had gone. It was replaced the following morning by another. The Queen wanted to know why.

In her late years, Queen Victoria had grown very fond of John Brown, her Balmoral gillie and personal attendant. She knew of his proclivity for whisky and arranged for a bottle to be placed each night in some out-of-the-way cupboard for his private consumption. No one had thought to bring this odd tradition to the notice of the Comptroller of the Household after the old Queen's death and the servants had continued to benefit from her thoughtfulness for fifty years.

Despite her stern and rather forbidding exterior, Queen Victoria could be surprisingly tolerant. Her subjects did not always follow her example. One of the most irascible was Sir William Eden, Bart. the father of Sir Anthony Eden, British prime minister at the time of Suez. On one occasion, Sir William came down to breakfast, pausing to tap the barometer in the hall. It was a particularly rainy morning, but for all his efforts the barometer continued to forecast bright sunshine. Sir William gathered it in his arms, marched to the front door and threw it down the steps, muttering: 'Go on, you damned fool, go and see for yourself'.

Another nasty morning, he went out on to the steps, shook his fist at the clouds and shouted: 'Just *like* you, God!'

Chapter 10

The Last Englishman

In its obituary in May 1966, the Daily Express described Lieutenant-Colonel Alfred Daniel Wintle M.C. as 'a real corpse-reviver who took more boredom out of life in the 1950's and 1960's than any other man in Britain.'

This is not quite the way *The Times* chose to express it, but it is nonetheless true. A self-appointed avenger of injustice, hypocrisy and pomposity, he said that he had fought clots all his life and expected to die of one. A fervent patriot who nightly thanked God for making him English, he prided himself that in a long life his monocle had always remained firmly in place, no matter how desperate the circumstance; and that he had only once unfurled his umbrella – to insert a note reading: 'This umbrella has been stolen from Colonel A. D. Wintle'.

'Mad Jack' Wintle was born at Mariupol in southern Russia on the last day of September 1897, the son of a British diplomat. His first memory was of Christmas, to which he looked forward with great anticipation. The reality proved to be an anticlimax. On his way to bed on Christmas night, he took a pencil and wrote 'Goodbye Christmas' on an obscure part of the ceiling, halfway up the stairs. It remained there for years, a permanent reminder of what Christmas ought to be, but wasn't. He was not punished for this misdemeanour because it was not discovered. But he was punished for everything else. His father was a martinet, a fierce blustering sort of man, who beat his children with a big stick for the smallest offence. AD loved him but admitted, in later life, that his one reservation about dying was the thought that the old bully might still be wielding his big stick 'in some celestial quarter'.

He was an intelligent boy with a natural aptitude for languages. He quickly became proficient in French and German, both of which were later to stand him in good stead. Even as a child his patriotism was very marked and he confided to his diary that there were essentially two classes of Englishmen: those who believed themselves superior to foreigners; and those who *knew* they were.

He formed an early dislike for the Germans and was therefore very upset when in 1910 he was sent to school at Neuwied am Rhein. He revenged himself by undermining authority with a series of practical jokes. It was a rule that if the temperature in the schoolroom exceeded 25 degrees centigrade by mid-morning, all classes were cancelled for the day. AD took to reflecting sunlight onto the thermometer by way of a small pocket mirror with the result that the school soon became the hottest place in Europe.

By the summer of 1915, England was at war with Germany and any last vestiges of affection which the young Wintle might have felt for his former companions had evaporated. He pestered his father to allow him to enter the Royal Military Academy at Woolwich – known to its inmates as 'The Shop' – as a gentleman cadet. In order to understand the intensity of his desire, it is necessary to examine the reasons for the creeping paralysis which had blighted the war and the attitude of the generals who conducted it.

Undermined at home by the meddlesome policies of Lloyd George and restricted by the terrain from using the bold, sweeping tactics which had stood the British army in such good stead in the past, Haig and his fellow generals were forced to wage a war of attrition. Aided and abetted by inept strategy, the cost in human life was terrifying. At Passchendale a quarter of a million men were killed or seriously injured; at Ypres, fifty thousand. At the battle of the Somme, fifty-eight thousand British soldiers were put out of action on the first day; and at the end of four months, and having advanced just eight miles, that number had risen to half a million. The survivors claimed to have added an inch to their height by the constant effort required in lifting their boots from the mud.

At Arras the generals lost one hundred and sixty thousand men in the course of advancing the allied position five miles. The losses in this one battle alone were five times greater than all the troops deployed in the Crimea War. Placed end to end, one hundred and sixty thousand dead would have formed a gruesome queue a hundred and seventy-four miles long. Small wonder that Lloyd George said: 'We could beat the Germans if we could only get Haig to lead them'.

Typical of the generals who had charge of the army when Wintle first entered it. Haig was the scion of a famous family of whisky distillers – Scottish lairds who could trace their descent back to the brigands and robbers who settled the border country in the thirteenth century. Educated at Clifton, Oxford and Sandhurst, he entered the army by way of a commission in the Seventh Hussars. By instinct a plodder, he rose to command without ever grasping the fundamentals of leadership and his ignorance of any world beyond his own was profound. This was illustrated by a remark which he made to a group of war correspondents: 'I think I understand . . . you want to get hold of little stories of heroism and so forth and to write them up in a bright way to make good reading for Mary Anne in the kitchen and the man in the street'.

It is not the substance of the remark which chills – it was probably a very shrewd estimation of what many of the journalists did want – but the formula by which he reduced ordinary people to a cypher. It was said that Kitchener had never spoken to an ordinary soldier. From his conversation, it could be doubted whether Haig had ever spoken to a civilian.

Although 'The Shop' was 'a small hell on earth' compared to which Haig's Sandhurst seemed like 'a home for cripples', Wintle managed to get himself passed out in a record four months. He was commissioned in the Royal Garrison Artillery and sent to the Western Front. Within minutes of his arrival the Germans unleashed an artillery bombardment. The noise was indescribable and the destruction beyond belief. Wintle saw the young sergeant standing next to him blown to pieces. He was so frightened that he could neither move nor speak. He forced himself to stand rigidly to attention for thirty seconds. At the end of that period: 'I was able to become again an Englishman of action and to carry out calmly the duties I had been trained to perform'. It had been a lucky escape, the first of many. A few months later, while acting as Forward Observing Officer in the attack on Girshy, a sniper's bullet 'removed one of my shoulder straps as neatly as a tailor could'.

At the third battle of Ypres in July 1917, as he was helping to manoeuvre a horsedrawn eighteen-pounder across muddy terrain, one of the wheels struck a mine. Wintle woke up in hospital minus his left eye and with the sight of his right eye so impaired that he was never able to see out of it again without the use of a monocle. He also lost 'a kneecap, five-and-a-half fingers and one-and-a-quarter thumbs'. As soon as he was able to withstand the journey, he was shipped home. He was nineteen years old and it was generally assumed that his fighting days were over.

He was sent for a period of convalescence to the Southern General Hospital at Oxford, but was soon making secret plans to return to France. The night before he proposed to leave, he learned that the nurses were holding a ladies-only dance. He attended this wearing a sister's uniform. As he had forgotten to remove his monocle, he was soon unmasked by Matron.

The following morning, he encountered Matron again. Shortly after dawn, as he was preparing to make his escape, she looked into his room, became suspicious and ran off to raise the alarm. By the time she returned he had gone.

Characteristically, even in flight, Wintle had taken great care with his appearance, pressing, rubbing and burnishing until every aspect of his turnout was immaculate. Aboard the train which was to take him on the first leg of his journey to France, he noticed that the elderly gentleman sitting opposite was unable to take his eyes off him. Wintle was still basking in his regard when the man leaned forward and said: 'I hope you don't mind me mentioning it, but your fly-buttons are undone'.

On the following Monday, Wintle returned to France where, on 4th November 1918 near Jolentz, he captured thirty-five prisoners single-handed. Although he afterwards claimed that he was kept so busy in the concluding weeks of the war that he was unable to recall it, this extraordinary feat of bravery earned him the Military Cross.

On Armistice Day 1918, he began his private preparations for World War Part Two. He refused to believe that the Germans were really beaten, describing the 'Kaiser's War' as one episode in a two-act drama. 'The filthy Boche' had sued for peace merely in order to preserve their strength. These views led many of his brother officers to shun him and for the next twenty years he was treated as something of a crank.

As he had returned to France without permission, he now left it in the same manner. Thanks to the continuing influence of his diplomat father, he was put to work in the German section of the War Office. It might have been expected that his intimate knowledge of the language would prove of benefit. But his strong sense of purpose and abrasive manner rendered him unpopular. In 1920 he was posted to Ireland as Head of Military Intelligence, Limerick Brigade Area.

Although this was Ireland at the time of The Troubles, life seems to have been relatively tranquil. A passionate equestrian – his first act on regaining consciousness after being blown up in 1917 had been to enquire after the horses – Wintle spent his time hacking across country in the knowledge that 'time spent dismounted can never be regained'. At the end of the year he applied to be transferred to a Cavalry regiment and was posted to the Eighteenth Royal Hussars at Secunderabad.

India was then still a far-flung outpost of the British Empire and the prevailing atmosphere owed much to its late Viceroy, the grandiloquent Lord Curzon, who is said to have gone everywhere 'as if accompanied by elephants'. Because Curzon had such a powerful influence in moulding the attitudes and opinions of men like Wintle – and because he was himself something of an eccentric – we must pause for a moment to examine his career.

Born with a head so disproportionately broad and heavy that as a child it caused him to overbalance at the top of a flight of stairs, Lord Curzon was haunted all his life by the early nickname of 'Moonface'; and by a contemptuous piece of burlesque verse composed by an Eton schoolmate:

My name is George Nathaniel Curzon
I am a most superior person.
My cheek is pink, my hair is sleek.
I dine at Blenheim once a week.

He was a compulsive worker and a prolific writer of letters. This led Sir Herbert Tree to remark: 'I will not go so far as to say that all people who write letters of more than eight pages are mad; but it is a curious fact that madmen never write letters of *less* than eight pages'.

Curzon's first marriage – to an American heiress – was idyllic. His second wife, Grace, eventually fell out of love with him. He quarelled with his daughters over the autocratic and cavalier manner in which he had administered their mother's estate; and his tempestuous affair with the romantic novelist Elinor Glyn ended in bitterness and disillusion. In old age he became very lonely and is said to have diverted himself 'by listening to the servants talking on the house telephone'.

A few years before Wintle arrived in India, a power struggle developed between Curzon and the head of the army, Lord Kitchener. The two men fell to squabbling over the administration of the country like a pair of feudal nabobs. Curzon threatened to resign unless Kitchener was recalled to England. It was a disastrous miscalculation. As far as the British government was concerned, the Viceroy was dispensable. Lord Kitchener was not: his recall would have provoked a national outcry. Curzon's tentatively proffered resignation was accepted with almost indecent alacrity; and when he attempted to withdraw it he was told that as the King had been informed, the decision was irrevocable.

The experience etched itself deep on his soul. He never again resigned office, preferring for the remainder of his political life to cling to power no matter how humiliating the consequences or how many coats it was necessary to turn in order to do so. In May 1923, when the premiership fell vacant, he was passed over for the less able Baldwin – ostensibly because he was a member of the House of Lords. In fact, it was feared that his overweening pride and total inability to delegate would destroy both himself and the office.

Although he had been appointed Viceroy at the early age of thirty-nine, and although he introduced numerous reforms and restored many ancient buildings – including the Taj Mahal – the army was pleased to see the back of him. He was not their kind of man. In the end, he was not anyone's kind of man. 'Chips' Channon attended his funeral and wrote in his diary:

> Where were the royalties he had served? Where were the statesmen he had made and terrified? Where were the Oriental potentates he had cowed? Where were the companions of his Oxford days? No one. Only the Duke of Devonshire, who had come over from Chatsworth and our little group from London.

The era of autocratic privilege personified by Curzon did not end with his removal. Life for the army continued to be very pleasant. Officers entertained one another royally in the mess; exercised their horses; took extended periods of leave, which they spent in exotic hotels or in England; played endless games of polo; indulged their passion for pig-sticking; and went on special courses devised to keep them occupied and amused.

One day, Wintle's name appeared in general orders to attend an intelligence course, the highlight of which was an initiative exercise aimed at discovering the exact location, security arrangements, layout, contents and staff numbers of a military arsenal. As anyone spotted by the course Observer would automatically lose marks, it was necessary to adopt disguise.

Wintle listened to the instructions and took himself off to his club where he ordered a cocktail known as a Blue Nile. He contacted a colleague at Command H.Q. and acquired a map of the depot. This, together with a local commercial directory and 'The Armaments Year Book', provided him with all the information he needed. His companions armed themselves with compasses, binoculars and field rations. They then descended on the arsenal, crawling about in the midday sun in a series of ludicrous disguises. AD played a game of billiards against his left hand, went for a swim, had a haircut and treated himself to an excellent lunch.

The following day, each officer's performance was examined in turn. One had attempted to breach the perimeter security by disguising himself as a washerwoman. As he forgot to remove his spurs, he was quickly spotted. A second man bribed a coolie to wheel him into the depot in a wheelbarrow, tied up in a sack. The sentry on duty disbelieved the coolie's statement that the sack contained firewood and smashed down on it several times with the butt of his rifle. The officer ended up in hospital.

With the exception of Wintle, all the officers had either been apprehended or observed. Having treated them to a contemptuous tongue-lashing, the C.O. turned to Wintle and asked how he alone had managed to furnish such a detailed report without being seen. Wintle told the exact truth. He had not been near the arsenal – did not have the faintest idea where it was.

After a moment's silence, the C.O. said: 'Mr Wintle's methods exactly embody the principles which I have been endeavouring to instill in you. His first object was to produce a report. He has produced it. His second object was not to be seen. He wasn't. His third was not to ask questions. He didn't'.

In 1923, and as the result of a regimental amalgamation, Wintle was posted to Cologne. As the polo season was then about to get under way, he managed to borrow or buy several ponies which he stabled in a set of outhouses officially reserved for the use of the Commanding Officer, a man known as 'Old Magoo'. Some weeks later, Old Magoo happened to visit the stables and was shocked to see his own groom vigorously brushing down 'Mr Wintle's polo ponies'. He was even more shocked to hear the man describe himself as 'Mr Wintle's polo manager'. He rushed back to his office and ordered Lieutenant Wintle to remove the ponies 'as soon as possible'.

As Wintle was the first to appreciate, 'as soon as possible' is an elastic term. He made half-hearted attempts to sell some of them, but not until the season was over. When Old Magoo made a further inspection, there were still five horses in the stables and he ordered AD to remove these within twenty-four hours. Two were quickly sold. The remainder had been borrowed from the Chief Remount Officer who was loath to take them back unless he could first allocate them elsewhere. Wintle suggested the C.O.

The next day Old Magoo stormed into Wintle's quarters. 'What the devil do you mean by it, sir?' he roared. 'I thought I told you to remove all your ponies from my stable within twenty-four hours.' Wintle quietly confirmed that he had done so. 'You have not, sir. I have just seen three of 'em with my own eyes.' Wintle said that they were not his ponies. Old Magoo was now near to apoplexy. 'Not yours, sir?' he raged. 'Not yours? Then who in God's name do they belong to?' Wintle said: 'To you, sir'.

He never tired of this Bilkoesque type of behaviour. One day a young and rather snobbish subaltern mentioned that for fourteen years his great uncle had been chief anaesthetist at St Thomas's Hospital. Turning to Wintle, he added: 'Not that I expect you know what an anaesthetist is'. Wintle said: 'Yes I do. He's one of those damned fellows who won't believe in God'.

He was also amused by people who chose to refer to themselves anatomically – as 'the eyes and ears of the regiment' or so-and-so's 'right hand man'. But he was quick to point out that he had never found anyone prepared to admit to being 'the arse of Kent County Council' or 'the genital organ of the *Glasgow Bugle*'.

Late in 1923, Wintle was posted to first the Royal Dragoons, the oldest, most prestigious Regiment of the Line, founded in 1661. A year later, he broke his leg in a riding accident and was removed to Aldershot Military Hospital. Here he made the acquaintance of Boy Mays, a trumpeter with the Royal Dragoons Band. Boy Mays was suffering from mastoiditis and diphtheria. He was not expected to live and had been removed to a part of the ward known colloquially as 'Stiffs' Retreat'.

As soon as he was able to hobble about, AD approached the lad and in typical ride-'em-down-roughshod fashion, said: 'What's all this nonsense about dying, Mays? You know it is an offence for a Royal Dragoon to die in bed. You will stop dying at once. And when you get up – get your bloody hair cut'. In 1959, when AD became the subject of a 'This Is Your Life' programme, Cedric Mays confided to Eamonn Andrews: 'After that I was too terrified to die'.

On a further spell of regimental duty in India, AD contracted septicaemia and was taken to hospital at Poona where he found himself in a ridiculous situation. The doctors told him that unless he returned to England he would almost certainly die. As it was impossible to return to England except on leave – and as it was impossible to obtain leave unless the doctor pronounced you fit – it appeared that he would breathe his last at Poona. He did eventually persuade the Chief Medical Officer to give him a clean bill of health; but shortly before he was due to embark received a top-priority telegram marked 'Urgent' and 'Secret'. Fearing that it contained something which would delay his departure, he destroyed it unopened. He never did discover its contents.

Wintle had now been an active soldier for ten years and was beginning to yearn for a permanent home. He bought a beautiful seventeenth century cottage at Wrotham, in the Weald of Kent, and occupied the next few months in doing it up, erecting a flagpole in the garden from which he flew the flag of The Royals.

In 1931 he was appointed instructor at St Cyr, the French Staff College. He remained there until 1935. His unbridled Englishness caused the cadets to sneer at him and to claim that England was finished. Wintle feared they were right.

Germany under Hitler was feverishly rearming, yet the War Office and the politicians continued to bleat that another confrontation so soon after the last was unthinkable. Wintle compared this attitude to that of the man 'whose house burned down, who received payment from his insurance company and then immediately cancelled cover on the grounds that it is impossible to be unlucky twice'. The 'bloody Boche', he said, 'are like their dogs: they cannot be trusted. The wolf will out.' His belief that Chamberlain was Hitler's dupe, and that Germany was preparing for war even while it attempted to placate its ancient enemy with false promises of peace, only served to confirm the War Office's opinion that it was dealing with a dangerous, obsessive crank.

Wintle's opinion of the War Office mandarins was equally unflattering. They were traitors – traitors who would allow the greatest country in the world to lose a war by default rather than jeopardise their safe jobs and pensions. On 3rd September 1939 Wintle was proved right and Whitehall was proved wrong. Chamberlain declared war on Germany.

Fortunately, there were still a few people in positions of authority prepared to employ a man who believed in 'always doing something positive' and in December Wintle was entrusted with the task of flying to France to discover from General Gamelin how long that country might reasonably be expected to hold out. Over dinner, Gamelin said: 'England is letting us down'. Wintle broke down and wept. The following day he met General Mendigal, Chief of Staff to the French Air Force, who made him promise that in the event of a

German victory, he would fly to France at a moment's notice and try to salvage something of the country's air strength.

In this, however, he had reckoned without the power of the official mind and its slavish attachment to 'the proper channels'. On 1st June 1940, when it became apparent that France was lost, and knowing that the authorities would frown on such a mission, he attempted to commandeer an aircraft by representing himself as a senior Staff Officer needing to fly immediately to Bordeaux under conditions of absolute secrecy.

The airport commander became suspicious and telephoned the Air Ministry for confirmation. There was the most appalling row and AD was taken before the Director of Intelligence, a man named Boyle. He implored him, as a patriot, to allow him to undertake the venture. 'It is blood that is flowing in France,' he said 'not ink.' Boyle coldly informed him that he must not only remain in England but would almost certainly be court-martialled. Wintle drew his revolver and waving it under Boyle's nose, shouted: 'You and your kind ought to be shot'. He then returned to his unit, where he was shortly afterwards arrested.

An officer from the Lancashire Fusiliers was entrusted with the task of escorting him to the Tower of London. He was a nervous individual who kept searching his pockets in order to ensure that he had not mislaid the committal document. By the time they arrived at their destination, the thing was nowhere to be found. Wintle raised his eyes heavenwards and said: 'For God's sake, wait here. I'll go and get another. He did – and in the absence of a senior officer, signed it himself, using the Fusilier's back as a desk.

The authorities at the Tower realised that Wintle was not a traitor and made his life as comfortable as possible. He was allocated quarters with a telephone and a bathroom. A batman brought him his daily whisky exactly on the stroke of twelve o'clock.

After a few weeks, the War Office decided that a court-martial would not be in the country's best interest and offered him his freedom. Like George Francis Train before him, AD refused. He said that if the authorities set such store by 'the proper channels', they should not complain if others chose to do likewise.

The court-martial was held at the Duke of York's Barracks at Chelsea. When Wintle announced his intention of naming everyone he considered 'ought to be shot' for failing in their duty in the months leading up to the outbreak of war, the court attempted to silence him. Discovering that this was illegal, it reduced the twelve charges against him to one and sentenced him to a severe reprimand. Wintle said: 'I was almost disappointed'.

The government did ultimately attempt to salvage something from the wreck of the French Air Force – but by then it was too late.

Shortly after the court-martial, AD embarked for the Middle East. In the autumn of 1941 he was recalled and again sent to France, this time as an undercover agent charged with discovering the true conditions under which British prisoners of war were being held in the concentration camps. In order to do so, he adopted the disguise of a down-at-heel French schoolmaster. It was the supreme sacrifice. As he said himself: 'Could a gentleman do more for England than dress like this?'

Although his outfit seems to have aroused a certain amount of suspicion, he reached Marseilles after a sea-journey of eight days. He was forced to share his cabin throughout with two villainous Frenchmen. Fortunately, his French was immaculate. Had it not been 'they would undoubtedly have shot me there and then and dropped me overboard'. On arrival: 'I had to go through fourteen different departments before I was fully documented for life in Vichy France'. Small wonder that he smiled when he heard the motto the French Resistance had bestowed on the collaborationist regime: 'Veni, Vidi, Vichy – I came, I saw, I concurred'.

For two weeks, AD amassed a wealth of information on life in occupied France, some of which eventually reached Wavell in Cairo. He stayed at a waterside hotel, buying what he needed on the black market with money acquired by selling the small quantity of gold which he had smuggled into the country strapped under his armpits.

On the seventeenth day he was instructed to make contact with a Frenchman who would furnish him with information regarding British prisoners of war. The Frenchman turned out to be a double agent and Wintle was arrested. He was taken to a prison at Toulon where he was kept for weeks in a dark, unsanitary cell and fed on scraps. His weight shrunk to seven stone and he briefly contemplated suicide. When he realised with what general rejoicing the news of this would be received in Whitehall, he abandoned the idea and resolved to escape.

The door to his cell was fastened by a stout lock. The hinges, however, were old, rusted and capable of being removed with relative ease. One night, he simply prised the door loose and escaped across the battlements. He walked for three days, eventually reaching the house of a man he believed would help him. He had hardly washed the accumulated grime from his face, however, before the police arrived and rearrested him. Denouncing his captors for 'swivel-eyed sons of syphilitic slime-frogs', he replaced his monocle and returned to his cell in Toulon.

He decided that if he could not immediately escape, he would at least 'do something positive'. His warders were a shabby bunch of dispirited collaborationists who had allowed their appearance to degenerate beyond all acceptable military standards. Knowing that 'the French are extremely vulnerable to insult', AD announced that he would not eat again until they smartened themselves up – cleaned their buttons, polished their boots and undertook to shave at least once a day. Against all the odds, they responded to a man.

Wintle's satisfaction was short-lived. News of his existence had reached the Germans who were lobbying for him to be shot as a spy.

Escape was now imperative. Using one of the springs from his bed, he laboriously cut through an inch-thick iron bar which impeded access to a narrow passageway down which the refuse cart passed each week. The next time it called he hurled himself into it, burrowing deep into the foul-smelling contents. After a cursory inspection, the cart trundled out through the main gate and 'the Galloping Major' was free. This time he decided to seek help from no one. Moving only under cover of darkness, he eventually reached the border with Spain and from there returned to England.

Nearly twenty years later, the period he had spent in captivity at Toulon was furnished with a fitting postscript when the Commander of the prison garrison, a man named Molia, came forward to pay tribute to his gallant prisoner on 'This Is Your Life'. He said:

> Shortly after Colonel Wintle left us I was moved – entirely because of his dauntless example and his tirade of abuse and challenge – to defect from Vichy. I took two hundred and eighty men from the

prison garrison – most of whom had been inspired by the Colonel or shamed by him – and joined the Resistance. Many of my men were later killed fighting the Germans but we harried and did down the enemy for years as Colonel Wintle would have wanted us to do.

At the end of an eventful war, Colonel Wintle resigned his commission and settled down to the life of a country gentleman. He married a lady whom he had known for thirty years and he devoted himself to his garden. His days of military adventure were over. His days of civil adventure were just beginning.

In 1948 Alfred Daniel Wintle locked horns with the law in a dispute which was to last ten years and bring him to the verge of bankruptcy. The cause of the trouble was his second cousin, a lady named Kitty Wells, who had died the previous year leaving a quite extraordinary will.

Kitty was a wealthy spinster who divided her time between a house in Orpington and another in Hove. She was timid, reclusive and rather feeble-minded. She had come to believe that her brother's divorce had damaged the family reputation beyond repair and in order to convince the postman and neighbours at Hove of her own respectability she had developed the odd habit of sending 'letters' to herself, bulky envelopes stuffed with old bus tickets, which she afterwards stored under her bed.

Wintle's sister, Marjorie, had lived with Kitty for more than a quarter of a century, acting as unpaid secretary, nurse and companion. Kitty was deeply attached to Marjorie, but relied for everyday advice on her solicitor, an eminently 'respectable' but totally unscrupulous Brighton man named Frederick Nye. She constantly deferred to his opinions and, although she was worth more than a hundred thousand pounds, refused to make even the most inconsequential purchase on the grounds that: 'Mr Nye tells me I cannot afford it'.

Nye capitalised on his client's fear that the scandalous details of her brother's divorce might any day be resurrected in the press, to order her affairs to his own advantage. He also played upon her sense of shame to isolate her from her friends.

The measure to which he succeeded in this was demonstrated one afternoon when a pedestrian accidentally knocked against the bonnet of Wintle's stationary car. The young man was not hurt, admitted that he was entirely to blame and apologised profusely. Kitty, however, was reduced to tears. 'Does it mean a court case?' she said. 'Does it mean all that dreadful business will be made public again?'

This and similar incidents persuaded Wintle to broach the subject of Marjorie's future. He pointed out that she had devoted herself to Kitty for many years. Perhaps the time had come for her to pursue a career of her own. Kitty would not hear of it. 'Marjorie' she said 'has been well provided for.' Being a gentleman, Wintle left it at that.

But when Kitty died, it transpired that she had assigned the bulk of her estate to Frederick Nye. Marjorie was to receive a bequest of forty pounds.

Marjorie accepted this with philosophical good humour. Her brother did not. He obtained a copy of the will which was couched in phrases so complex and obscure that even Wintle's solicitor could not unravel them. It had been drawn up by the chief beneficiary and witnessed by two of his clerks.

In the hope of negotiating an amicable settlement, Wintle began by appealing to Nye's better nature. Nye returned his letters unopened, refused to see him or accept his telephone calls. Wintle next decided to harass him by publishing a series of calculated insults in the press. He showed one of these letters to a legal friend, who said: 'Good God, man. He's got to prosecute you for criminal libel. If he doesn't, he's a crook'.

Nye did not prosecute. Faced with this wall of silence, but holding firm to his belief in 'always doing something positive, even if it's wrong', Wintle settled on a desperate course of action. Pretending to be an important client, he lured the solicitor to a hired flat, stripped him at pistol-point of his trousers and made him stand in a corner in his long-johns, wearing on his head a dunce's cap fashioned from newspapers. He then took a picture of him and sent him home – minus his trousers.

He had at last achieved the required result. Later that evening the police descended on the Don Quixote of Wrotham and arrested him in his cottage.

The case was heard at Lewes Assizes in July 1955. In the hope of obtaining maximum publicity, Wintle tried to ventilate the grievance which had motivated the offence. The court refused to hear him.

Although Wintle was receiving a one hundred percent disability pension, and was clearly unwell, the Judge insisted that he could not overlook the gravity of the crime. He accepted that he had not intended any serious or lasting injury to Mr Nye – but he had nonetheless subjected a seventy-one-year-old man to a distressing and degrading ordeal at the point of a gun. He was sent to prison for six months.

As Wintle later pointed out, on the same day two other men were each fined £10 for assaults on little girls, while a third was fined a similar sum for beating a dog to death.

'Colonel Bogey' – as he was now dubbed by the popular press – served his time with characteristic insouciance. During the seven weeks he spent in Wormwood Scrubs he received more than two hundred letters of sympathy and support. He passed the remaining weeks at Eastchurch prison and it was from there, four months from the date of sentence and having earned full remission for good behaviour, that he was released. He was met at the gate by a friend who remarked that he must have found the experience a bit of a bore. AD said: 'I am never bored when I am around'.

Even in his darkest hour he had never considered abandoning his crusade and he now intensified the campaign to obtain some measure of justice for his sister. This time he utilised 'the proper channels'. Assisted by Cedric Mays – who had been 'frightened' back to life by Wintle more than thirty years earlier – he constructed a detailed dossier on the activities of Frederick Nye and prosecuted him in the High Court.

The trial lasted for more than a week. At the end of it, the legal profession was seen to have closed ranks. Judgement was given in favour of Nye. The Judge ordered Wintle to pay the costs, saying: 'As Colonel Wintle has dragged Mr Nye into court in order to expose him he ought to pay for his pleasure'.

Outraged by the decision, AD appealed. Again the court found in favour of Nye. At this point, Wintle resolved to carry the issue to the highest court in the land – the House of Lords. He jettisoned the lawyers who had been acting on his behalf, deciding to represent himself.

In order to see the thing through, he was forced to mortgage his last possessions. He was now a pauper; but at least he was an *English* pauper. He was sustained by his wife and by the support of his friends, notably Dame Sybil Thorndike and her husband, Sir Lewis Casson. With the help of Cedric Mays he supplemented the file on Nye until it ran with index to two hundred and fifty-three pages. They could not afford to have it printed and typed up the required forty-three copies themselves. It was hard, painstaking work, but this was the last redoubt: if they lost now they lost everything and for ever.

The case lasted six days and Wintle was on his feet for three of them. At a critical moment, one of the judges leaned forward and said: 'Colonel Wintle, it is quite clear that no one in any of the courts has understood this will'. Wintle replied: 'Then it must be likely, with due respect, that the simple Miss Wells did not understand it either'.

The Times recorded the verdict under the headline: 'Cavalry Officer Jumps Last Fence to Win'. For the first time in the history of the English law, a layman had ventured into the House of Lords and emerged triumphant. Nye was required to forfeit all benefit under Kitty's will and to pay the costs.

Not long after this famous victory, AD and Cedric Mays were lunching at the Wig and Pen Club, at the western end of Fleet Street when the conversation turned to death. Wintle said that he would dearly love to have the band of the Royal Dragoons play Schubert's 'Serenade' at his funeral. Mays said he would do his best to arrange it.

In May 1966, as he had predicted he would, Colonel Wintle died of a clot. When Cedric Mays learned that the band of the Royal Dragoons was serving overseas and would not be available to play at the funeral, he drank a bottle of malt whisky, travelled to Canterbury Cathedral and standing stiffly to attention in the Chapel of the Cavalrymen of Great Britain sang 'the whole damned thing' himself.

Bibliography

Alderson, B. (1903), *Arthur James Balfour* (Grant Richards).
Altick, R. (1972), *Victorian Studies in Scarlet* (Dent).
Apperley, C. J. (1892), *Memoirs of the Life of the Late John Mytton* (Routledge and Sons).
Aubrey, J. (1813), *Lives of Eminent Men* (2 v.).
Bailey, J. (Ed.) (1927), *The Diary of Lady Frederick Cavendish Murray*.
Baily, L. (1973), *Gilbert and Sullivan and Their World* (Thames and Hudson).
Baldwin, A. W. (1955), *My Father: The True Story* (Allen and Unwin).
Balfour, A. J. (1879), *The Foundations of Belief* (Macmillan).
Ballou, A. R. (1964), *Personal Recollections of Norton I.*
Balsan, C. (1952), *The Glitter and the Gold* (Harper, New York).
Barker, E. H. (1852), *Porsonia.*
Barnes, A. G. (Ed.) (1927) *The Rehearsal by George Villiers, Duke of Buckingham and The Critic*, by Richard Brinsley Sheridan.
Barrow, A. (1978), *Gossip: 1920–1970* (Hamish Hamilton).
Bartlett, D. L. and Steele, J. B. (1979), *Empire: The Life, Legend and Madness of Howard Hughes* (Andre Deutsch).
Beadle, J. (1979), *Today's the Day* (W. H. Allen).
Bell, C. (1873), *Speech of C. Bell upon the enquiry into the Sanity of G. F. Train.*
Bennett, A. (1784), *Memoirs of a Welch Heiress* (4 v.) (Privately printed).
Benson, E. F. (1930), *A Victorian Peep Show* (Longman).
Beste, H. D. (1829), *Personal & Literary Memorials* (Henry Colburn).
Besterman, T. (1935), *The Druce-Portland Case* (Duckworth)
Blyth, H. (1967), *Old Q: The Rake of Piccadilly* (Weidenfeld & Nicolson).
Bordeaux, P. (1925), *The Circe of the Deserts* (Hurst & Blackett).
Boswell, J. (1901), *Life of Johnson* (Dent).
Boyle, J. (1752), *Remarks on the Life & Writings of Jonathan Swift.*
Bramah, E. (1972), *Tea & Coffee* (Hutchinson).
Brewer, E. C. (1975), *Dictionary of Phrase & Fable* (Cassell).
Bronowski, J. (1944), *A Man Without a Mask* (Secker & Warburg).
Brooke-Little, J. (1976) *The British Monarchy* (Batsford).
Brown, I. (1966), *Balmoral: A History of a Home* (Collins).
Bruce, I. (1951), *The Nun of Lebanon.*
Bryant, Sir Arthur (1937) *Stanley Baldwin: A Tribute* (Hamish Hamilton).
Burke, Sir John (1855), *The Romance of the Aristocracy* (Henry Colburn).
Burke, Sir John (1859), *Vicissitudes of Families* (Longman).
Burke, Sir John (1882), *Reminiscences, Ancestral, Anecdotal and Historic* (Longman).

Burney, F. (1931), *Diaries & Letters* (Routledge).
Burton, E. (1972), *The Early Victorians at Home* (Longman).
Bushell, P. (1983), *London's Secret History* (Constable).
Carlyle, T. (1881), *Reminiscences* (2 v.) (Longman).
Caro, J. (1864), *Lessing & Swift*.
Chancellor, E. B. (1924), *Lives of the Rakes* (6 v.) (P. Allan).
Channon, Sir Henry (1967), *Diaries* (Weidenfeld & Nicolson).
Chapman, G. T. (1937), *Life of Beckford* (Cape).
Chapman, G. T. (1928), *The Travel Diaries of William Beckford*.
Charteris, E. (1931), *Life of Gosse* (Heinemann).
Clark, R. W. (1968), *JBS: The Life & Work of J. B. S. Haldane*.
Clarke, W. (1809), *The Authentic & Impartial Life of Mary Anne Clarke*.
Clerici, C. (1907), *A Queen of Indiscretions: The Tragedy of Caroline of Brunswick* (John Lane, New York).
Cookridge, E. H. (1966), *From Battenburg to Mountbatten* (Barker).
Crocker, W. C. (1973), *Tales from the Coffee Houses* (Hale).
Curtis, G. (1972), *Queen Anne* (Weidenfeld & Nicolson).
Dancer, D. (1810), *The Strange & Unaccountable Life of Daniel Dancer*.
Darwin, B. (1943), *British Clubs* (Collins).
Davidson, H. F. (1935), *The Reason Why* (Privately printed).
Dearden, H. (1935), *Queer People* (Hutchinson).
De Cornuel (1728), *Lettres de Mlle. Aisse*.
Defoe, D. (1722), *A Journey Through England* (8 v.).
De Quincey, T. (1948), *Anne of Oxford Street* (Lighthouse Books).
De Quincey, T. (1822), *Confessions of an English Opium Eater* (Taylor & Hessey).
Dexter, T. (1838), *A Pickle for the Knowing Ones* (Otis, Broaders, Boston).
Dickinson, V. (Ed.) (1919), *Miss Eden's Letters* (Macmillan).
Dictionary of National Biography.
Dingwall, E. J. (1947), *Some Human Oddities* (Home & Van Thal).
Dobbs, D. (1972), *Drury Lane* (Cassell).
Donaldson, F. (1972), *The Actor Managers* (Weidenfeld & Nicolson).
Dowie, J. A. (1912), *The Personal Letters of John Alexander Dowie* (Wilbur Glenn Voliva, Zion City, Illinois).
Drury, E. and Bridgeman, H. (1975), *The British Eccentric* (Michael Joseph).
Eaton, H. A. (1936), *Thomas de Quincey* (Oxford University Press).
Eden, Sir Anthony (1976), *Another World: 1897–1917* (Allen Lane).
Emerson, R. W. (1844), *Essays* (The Catholic Series).
Emerson, R. W. (1850), *Representative Men* (Routledge).
Encyclopaedia Britannica.
Epton, N. (1962), *Milord and Milady* (Olbourne).
Epton, N. (1960), *The English in Love* (Cassell).
Esher, Viscount (1934), *Journals and Letters*.
Evans, B. (1947), *The Natural History of Nonsense* (Michael Joseph).
Evans, H. *Our Old Nobility*. Reprinted with additions from the *Echo* newspaper.
Fane, Lady Augusta (1926), *Chit-Chat* (Thornton Butterworth).
Frith, W. P. (1887), *My Autobiography & Reminiscences* (2 v.) (Bentley & Son).
Fulford, R. (1949), *The Prince Consort* (Macmillan).
Gammond, P. (1971), *Your Own, Your Very Own* (Ian Allen).

Gay, J. (1716), *Trivia*.
George, D. (Ed.) (1957), *The Book of Anecdotes* (Hulton Press).
Girtin, T. (1964), *The Abominable Clubman* (Hutchinson).
Godwin, T. (1809), *Essays on Sepulchres*.
Granger (1779), *History* (3 v.).
Graves, C. P. R. (1963), *Leather Armchairs* (Cassell).
Green, J. (1979), *Famous Last Words* (Omnibus Press).
Green, V. H. H. (1966), *The Hanoverians* (Arnold).
Greenwall, H. J. (1957), *Northcliffe* (Wingate).
Gribble, L. (1972), *More Famous Historical Mysteries* (Muller).
Gronow, Captain R. H. (1862) *Reminiscences*.
Guedalla, P. (1926), *Selected Essays* (Harrap).
Haldane, J. B. S. (1951), *Everything Has A History* (Allen & Unwin).
Hardy, J. G. (1972), *The Rise & Fall of the British Nanny* (Hodder & Stoughton).
Hare, A. (1900), *The Story of My Life* (Allen & Unwin).
Harington, Sir J. (1615) *Epigrams*.
Harlan, R. (1906), *John Alexander Dowie . . . and the church in Zion* (Wisconsin).
Harris, F. (1945), *My Life and Loves* (4 v.) (Obelisk Press, Paris).
Harris, L. (1965), *The Fine art of Political Wit* (Cassell).
Hawkins, Sir John (1962), *Life of Samuel Johnson* (Cape).
Haydon, B. R. (1877), *Correspondence & Table-Talk* (2 v.) (Chatto & Windus).
Hazlitt, W. (1830), *Conservations with James Northcote R.A.*
Historical Register.
Holcroft, T. (1816), *Memoirs of the Late Thomas Holcroft* (2 v.).
Holland, Lady (1855), *A Memoir of the Reverend Sydney Smith*, by his daughter, 2nd Edition.
Holloway, S. (1973), *London's Noble Fire Brigades 1833–1904* (Cassell).
Horn, P. (1975), *The Rise & Fall of the Victorian Servant* (Gill & Macmillan).
Huggett, F. E. (1977), *Life Below Stairs* (Murray).
Hughes, R. (1937), *Howard Hughes: Record Breaker* (Mafadden).
Huis, R. (1821), *Memoirs of Queen Caroline*.
Hutchins, J. H. (1940), *Jonas Hanway* (S.P.C.K.).
Ikbal, A. S. S. (1933), *The Tragedy of Amanullah*.
Jackson, S. (1968), *The Sassoons* (Heinemann).
John, E. (1933), *Charles I* (Barker).
Johnson, S. (1905), *Lives of the English Poets* (3 v.).
Judd, D. (1973), *The Life & Times of George V*. (Weidenfeld & Nicolson).
Kelly, M. (1826), *Reminiscences* (2 v.).
Kennedy, A. L., *Old Diplomacy & New*.
Kennedy, A. L., *Salisbury*.
King, Dr, *Anecdotes of His Own Time*.
King, R. A. (1895), *Swift in Ireland*.
Knapp, S. L. (1838), *Life of Timothy Dexter* (Boston).
Laver, J. (1961), *Between the Wars* (Vista Books).
Lejeune, A. and Lewis, M. (1979), *The Gentlemen's Clubs of London* (Macdonald and Janes)
Leslie, A. and Chapman, P. (1978), *Madame Tussaud* (Hutchinson).
Lindsay, P. (1951), *The Loves of Florizel (George IV)* (Hutchinson).

Liverpool, Lord Russell of (1967), *Caroline: the Unhappy Queen* (Hale).
Lloyd, A. (1971), *The Wickedest Age* (David & Charles).
Longford, Lady Elizabeth (1971), *Wellington* (2 v.) (Weidenfeld & Nicolson).
Lowndes, B. (1948), *A Passing World* (Macmillan).
Ludovic, L. J. (1962), *The Itch for Play* (Jarrolds).
Macaulay, Lord (1843), *Essays* (3 v.).
Macqueen-Pope, W. (1972), *Goodbye Piccadilly* (David & Charles).
Macqueen-Pope, W. (1971), *Ghosts & Greasepaint* (Hale).
Macqueen-Pope, W. (1957), *Give Me Yesterday* (Hutchinson).
Mallett, M. (1968), *Life With Queen Victoria* (Murray).
Margetson, S. (1969), *Leisure & Pleasure in the Nineteenth Century* (Cassell).
Marsh, Sir Edward (1939), *A Number of People* (Heinemann).
Masters, B. (1975), *Dukes* (Blond & Briggs).
Mathison, R. (1978), *The Secret Life of Howard Hughes* (Hale).
Melville, L. (1906), *The First Gentleman of Europe* (2 v.) (Hutchinson).
Melville, L. (1929), *In the Days of Queen Anne* (Hutchinson).
Melville, L. (1912), *An Injured Queen: Caroline of Brunswick* (Hutchinson).
Melville, L. (1910), *The Life & Letters of William Beckford* (Heinemann).
Melville, L. (1926), *Regency Ladies* (Hutchinson).
Melville, L. (1914), *Some Eccentrics & a Woman* (Martin Secker).
Miles, A. C. (1937), *Mosley in Motley* (A. C. Miles).
Mitchison, N. (1973), *Small Talk* (Bodley Head).
Mitford, A. B. F., Baron Redesdale (1915), *Memories* (2 v.) (Hutchinson).
Mitford, A. B. F., Baron Redesdale (1917), *Further Memories* (Hutchinson).
Mitford, J. (1960), *Hons and Rebels* (Gollancz).
Mitford, J. (1963), *The American Way of Death* (Hutchinson).
Mitford, N. (1945), *The Pursuit of Love* (Hamish Hamilton).
Morah, P. (1979), *Restoration England* (Constable).
Morris, Sergeant T. (1845), *Recollections of Military Service.*
Mosley, Lady Diana (1977), *A Life of Contrasts* (Hamish Hamilton).
Mosley, L. (1960), *Curzon: The End of an Epoch* (Longmans).
Mosley, Sir Oswald (1939), *The Greater Britain* (Greater Britain Publications).
Mosley, Sir Oswald (1936), *Fascism: 100 Questions Asked and Answered* (Fascist Shilling Library).
Muggeridge, M. (1940), *The Thirties* (Hamish Hamilton).
Nelson, M. (1976), *Nobs and Snobs* (Gordon & Cremonesi).
Nevill, R. H. (1947), *London Clubs* (Chatto & Windus).
Nichols, J. (1780c.) *Anecdotes of Mr Hogarth.*
Nicolson, Sir Harold (1966), *Diaries and Letters* (3 v.) (Collins).
Notes and Queries
Pain, N. (1975), *George III at Home* (Eyre Methuen).
Pearsall, R. (1975), *Night's Black Angels* (Hodder and Stoughton).
Pearsall, R. (1973), *Edwardian Life & Leisure* (David and Charles).
Pearson, H. (1951), *Dizzy* (Methuen).
Pearson, H. (1956), *Beerbohm Tree* (Methuen).
Pearson, H. (1934), *The Smith of Smiths* (Hamish Hamilton).
Perrott, R. (1968), *The Aristocrats* (Weidenfeld and Nicolson).
Petrie, Sir Charles (1965), *Scenes of Edwardian Life* (Eyre and Spotiswoode).

Phelan, J. (1977), *Howard Hughes: The Hidden Years* (Collins).
Phillips, P. (1944), *Professor J. B. S. Haldane* (Daily Worker League).
Portland, 6th Duke of (1937), *Men Women and Things* (Faber).
Priestley, J. B. (1975), *The English* (Heinemann).
Pryce-Jones, D. (1978), *Unity Mitford* (Star Books).
Pullar, P. (1975), *Frank Harris* (Hamish Hamilton).
Reader's Digest (1975), *Reader's Digest Book of Strange Stories* (Reader's Digest Association).
Redding, C. (1863), *Memoirs of Remarkable Misers* (2 v.).
Redding, C. (1859), *Memoirs of William Beckford.*
Redding, C. (1866), *Past Celebrities Whom I have Known* (2 v.).
Robinson, J. R. (1894), *The Last Earls of Barrymore.*
Rogers, S. (1952), *The Table-Talk of Samuel Rogers* (Richards Press).
Romilly, E. M. S. (1937), *Boadilla* (Hamish Hamilton).
Romilly, E. M. S. and Romilly, G. S. B. (1935), *Out of Bounds.*
Roth, C. (1941), *The Sassoon Dynasty* (Robert Hale).
Rush, P. (1964), *The Book of Duels* (Harrap).
Rush, P. (1957), *Strange People* (Hutchinson).
Russell, G. W. E. (1904), *Collections & Recollections* (Smith, Elder).
Rutherford, G. G. M. (1857), *The Adventures & Intrigues of The Duke of Buckingham.*
Sanders, L. C. (1887), *Life of Sheridan.*
Sassoon, D. S. (1950), *A History of the Jews in Baghdad* (S. D. Sassoon).
Sassoon, E. D. & Co. (1888), *Some Queer Stories of Benjamin David Benjamin & Messrs E.D. Sassoon & Co.*
Sassoon, Sir Philip (1929), *The Third Route* (Heinemann).
Sassoon, S. L. (1937), *Memoirs of a Fox-Hunting Man* (Faber).
Sheridan, T. (1785), *Life of Jonathan Swift.*
Shovel, Sir Cloudesley (1707), *The Life and Glorious Actions of Sir Cloudesley Shovel, etc.* (Published anonymously).
Shovel, Sir Cloudesley (1708), *Secret Memoirs of the Life of Sir Cloudesley Shovel etc.* (Published by a Gentleman).
Sitwell, E. (1933), *The English Eccentrics* (Faber).
Sitwell, O. (1950), *Noble Essences & Courteous Revelations* (Macmillan).
Smith, J. T. (1818), *A Book for a Rainy Day.*
Smith, Sydney (1893), *Bon-mots of Sydney Smith & R. B. Sheridan* (Dent).
Smith, Sydney (1860), *The Wit & Wisdom of the Reverend Sydney Smith.*
Smythe, Dame Ethel (1938), *Maurice Baring* (Heinemann).
Smythe, W. (1840), *Memoir of Mr Sheridan.*
Speaight, R. (1970), *The Property Basket* (Collins & Harvel Press).
Spence, J. (1898 edition), *Anecdotes.*
Stead, W. T. (1898), *Gladstone.*
Stirling, A. M. W. (1956), *The Merry Wives of Battersea* (Hale).
Stirling, A. M. W. (1959), *Odd Lives* (Macmillan)
Sutherland, D. (1969), *Raise Your Glasses* (Macdonald).
Sutherland, J. (Ed.) (1975), *The Oxford Book of Literary Anecdotes* (Clarendon Press).
Sykes, C. S. (1982), *Black Sheep* (Chatto & Windus).
Tattam, H. (1852), *A Short Memoir of the late J. C. Neild* (Privately printed).
Tennyson, C. (1949), *Alfred Tennyson* (Macmillan).

Thomson, G. M. (1973), *Lord Castlerosse* (Weidenfeld).
Thornton, W. (1948), *The Nine Lives of Citizen Train* (Greenberg, New York).
Thrale, H. (1942), *Thraliana* (2 v.) (Clarendon Press).
Tidsall, E. E. P. (1939), *Wanton Queen*.
Timbs, J. (1866), *English Eccentrics & Eccentricities* (2 v.) (Richard Bentley).
Timbs, J. (1869), *Ancestral Stories*.
Timbs, J. (1869), *Club Life*.
Timbs, J. (1872), *Anecdote Lives of Wits & Humorists* (2 v.).
Timbs, J. (1860), *Anecdote Biography*.
Timbs, J. (1874), *Anecdote Lives of the Later Wits & Humorists* (2 v.).
Timbs, J. (1886), *Anecdotes About Authors & Artists* (Diprose & Bateman).
Timbs, J. (1886), *Anecdotes About Lawyers, Doctors & Parsons* (Diprose & Bateman).
Timbs, J. (1864), *A Century of Anecdote* (2 v.).
Timbs, J. (1886), *Club Life of London*.
Timbs, J. (1869), *Historic Ninepins*.
Toynbee, T. P. (1961), *Underdogs: Eighteen Victims of Society* (Weidenfeld & Nicolson).
Toynbee, T. P. (1954), *A Memoir of Esmond Romilly and Jasper Ridley in the Thirties* (Macgibbon & Kee).
Train, G. F. (1858), *Letters* (New York).
Train, G. F. (1862), *The Downfall of England* (Philadelphia).
Train, G. F. (1902), *My Life in Many States & In Foreign Lands* (Appleton).
Trench, C. C. (1964), *The Royal Malady* (Longmans).
Tschumi, G. (1954), *Royal Chef* (Kimber).
Turner, E. S. (1975), *Amazing Grace* (Michael Joseph).
Turner, E. S. (1962), *What the Butler Saw: Two Hundred & Fifty Years of the Servant Problem* (Michael Joseph).
Villiers, G. (1715), *The Works of George Villiers, 2nd Duke of Buckingham* (S. Briscoe).
Wallace, I. (1958), *The Square Pegs* (Hutchinson).
Wallace, I. (1956), *Fabulous Originals* (Longmans, Green).
Walpole, H. (1804), *Walpoliana* (2 v.) (Philips).
Walpole, H. (1819), *Letters to G. Montagu 1736–1770*.
Walpole, H. (1840), *Letters* (6 v.) (Richard Bentley & Sons).
Walpole, H. (1762–71), *Anecdotes of Painting* (4 v.).
Walpole, H. (1859), *Journals of the Reign of George III*.
Walpole, H. (1818), *Reminiscences* (2 v.).
Watson, J. S. (1861), *Life of Porson*.
Wild, R. G. (1932), *Amanullah, ex-King of Afghanistan* (Hurst & Blackett).
Winchester, S. (1981) *Their Noble Lordships* (Faber)
Wintle, Colonel A. D. (1968), *The Last Englishman* (Joseph)
Wintle, Colonel, A. D. (1961), *The Club* (Cassell).
Wilson, H. (1821), *The Book of Wonderful Characters* (3 v.).
Wilson, H. (1813), *The Eccentric Mirror* (4 v.) (J. & J. Cundee).
Wilson, H. (1839), *Memoirs*.
Wilson, J. (1973), *C.B.: The Life of Sir Henry Campbell-Bannerman* (Constable).
Wilson, J. H. (1954), *A Rake & His Times: George Villiers 2nd Duke of Buckingham*.
Wood, A. (1965), *The True History of Lord Beaverbrook*.

Index